ESL VIDEO LIBRARY

FOCUS ON THE ENVIRONMENT

SUSAN STEMPLESKI

REGENTS/PRENTICE HALL
Englewood Cliffs, New Jersey 07632

Acquisitions Editor: **Nancy L. Leonhardt**
Development Editor: **Stephanie Karras**
Editorial Assistance: **D. Andrew Gitzy, Terry TenBarge**
Production Editor: **Jan Sivertsen**
Prepress Buyer: **Ray Keating**
Manufacturing Buyer: **Lori Bulwin**
Cover Supervisor: **Marianne Frasco**
Cover Design: **Ruta Kysilewskyj**
Cover Photograph: **© 1992 Arthur Tilley/FPG International**
Interior Design: **Tom Nery**
Technical Support: **Molly Pike Riccardi**

Printed in the United States of America
10 9 8 7 6 5 4 3 2 1

ISBN 0-13-007097-1

Prentice-Hall International (UK) Limited, *London*
Prentice-Hall of Australia Pty. Limited, *Sydney*
Prentice-Hall Canada Inc., *Toronto*
Prentice-Hall Hispanoamericana, S.A., *Mexico*
Prentice-Hall of India Private Limited, *New Delhi*
Prentice-Hall of Japan, Inc., *Tokyo*
Simon & Schuster Asia Pte, Ltd., *Singapore*
Editora Prentice-Hall do Brasil, Ltda., *Rio de Janeiro*

TABLE OF CONTENTS

ACKNOWLEDGMENTS

I would like to express my appreciation to the people who have helped to make this book possible.

A very special thank you to John Fanselow, Professor of Language and Education at Teachers College, Columbia University, for his guidance and encouragement, and for what I have learned from him about materials development.

I am particularly grateful to Paul Arcario of LaGuardia Community College of the City University of New York and to Tracey Forrest of Baruch College of the City University of New York for lending me their ears and their insights.

Many thanks to the entire editorial staff at Regents/Prentice Hall, but especially to Nancy Leonhardt for providing me with the opportunity to write this book and for her limitless assistance, encouragement, and good cheer throughout the project. Particular thanks also to Stephanie Karras for her suggestions and painstaking editorial work.

A long overdue but very sincere thank you to my mother, Helen M. Sutter, and my friends Maureen Kenney Nobile, John Pettet, and Shannon Randall for their patience, understanding, and special help when it was needed.

Finally, I thank the Master of Arts candidates at Teachers College, Columbia University, my colleagues at the International English Language Institute of Hunter College of the City University of New York, and the hundreds of other teachers I have worked with in teacher training and development seminars around the world. From them, I have had countless opportunities to learn. To them, I dedicate this book.

INTRODUCTION

The ABC News ESL Video Library is a series of interactive, task-based integrated skills texts for adult learners of English as a second or foreign language. Each text is accompanied by a video, which contains the core presentation of language, and an instructor's manual, which includes an answer key as well as complete transcripts of all the video segments. This video series is unique in that it uses actual broadcast footage from internationally known *ABC News* programs such as *Business World, PrimeTime Live, 20/20, Nightline, The Health Show,* and *World News Tonight* to stimulate students' interest in timely topics presented by world-famous anchors and reporters. More important, these broadcast segments provide authentic language input in real situations—nothing has been staged or "set up" artificially. Instead, language instruction flows from the natural language used and is thus always presented and practiced in context.

Each of the texts (*Focus on Business, Focus on Innovators and Innovations, Focus on the Environment, Focus on Health,* and *Focus on American Culture*) presents lively topics that are of interest to international students and that relate to life in the United States and abroad. Students are encouraged to see U.S. culture in the context of the global village and to bring in their own cultural views to analyze and interpret the video segments.

The instruction utilizes an interactive approach, providing many opportunities for students to work in pairs, small groups, and teams. Students are encouraged to pool their knowledge and learn from one another. The teacher functions as a facilitator, guiding students through tasks that enable them to discover and learn on their own.

To make the videos easy to use, time codes have been included in the upper right-hand corner of the screen. These time codes are cross-referenced in the texts so that you can easily find your place on the video. This feature also makes it easier to replay sections you find particularly useful or difficult as many times as you want.

The materials for each segment are divided into five sections: Previewing, Global Viewing, Intensive Viewing, Language Focus, and Postviewing. The purpose of each section is as follows:

Previewing challenges students to predict what the segment will cover. This section also helps activate the students' schema and enables the teacher to know what background information students bring to class. This section also presents essential vocabulary that the students will need to know in order to understand the segment.

Global Viewing develops students' understanding of the key ideas presented in the segment. In this section, students' overall comprehension and ability to look for main ideas are stressed.

Intensive Viewing zeroes in on specific items for comprehension to prepare students for the Postviewing tasks. Students practice looking and listening for details in activities such as notetaking and cloze-type exercises.

Language Focus gives practice in vocabulary and expressions students will need to use to complete the Postviewing tasks. Occasionally, an interesting point of language structure from the video segment is reviewed and practiced.

Postviewing provides a wealth of additional materials, such as readings, graphs, and questionnaires, all related to the topic of the segment. The final tasks pull together all the language and content skills the students have practiced in the segment.

An additional feature of the videos is that all of the programs, with the exception of *The Health Show*, are closed-captioned. If you have access to a decoder (or if your television has the new decoder chip), you can open up the captions and see the written transcriptions of what the speakers are saying as they speak.

FOCUS ON THE ENVIRONMENT

Focus on the Environment consists of twelve authentic news reports, each focusing on a different environmental issue. The overall goal of the text is threefold: (1) to aid in comprehension of the video segment and the environmental issues presented; (2) to encourage critical thinking about these issues; and (3) to stimulate the use of the language presented on the video.

In the **Previewing, Global Viewing, Intensive Viewing**, and **Language Focus** sections, the content of the video is used as a springboard for a variety of viewing activities—including predicting, getting the main idea, focusing on details, and notetaking—and for exercises focusing on the specific vocabulary and expressions used by the various speakers. In some cases, students will watch the entire video before doing a specific exercise; in other cases (especially in the Intensive Viewing sections), students will be asked to watch and focus on a particular section of the video.

In the **Postviewing** section, a wide variety of tasks—such as debates, brainstorming, discussions, values clarification exercises, and writing assignments—encourage analysis and interpretation of environmental issues. During these activities, students have the opportunity to work together and examine the issues in the context of their own culture and experience, and to integrate the language and concepts presented on the video with their own points of view. The following is a summary of the various postviewing tasks presented in each segment of the text.

Unit 1: Plant and Animal Habitats

Segment & Topic	Functions in Postviewing Tasks
1 Little Being Done to Stop Animal and Plant Extinction	• Reading about and discussing endangered species • Completing a pie chart • Debating the issue of banning the ivory trade • Conducting a survey about endangered species • Writing a reaction • Clarifying values

Unit 1: Plant and Animal Habitats (continued)

Segment & Topic	Functions in Postviewing Tasks
2 Medicines of the Rain Forests Disappearing	• Reading about and discussing rain forests • Tapping into prior knowledge • Writing a biography • Conducting a poll about cutting down rain forests • Reaching a consensus about cutting down rain forests • Clarifiying values
3 Marjory Douglas, 98-Year-Old Environmentalist	• Discussing issues related to old age • Reading about and taking notes on the Florida Everglades • Writing a reaction • Interviewing an environmental activist • Researching famous environmentalists • Map reading • Making a schedule of one's typical day

Unit 2: Air, Land, and Water

Segment & Topic	Functions in Postviewing Tasks
4 EPA Says Ozone Depletion More Serious Than Thought	• Reading about and discussing the ozone layer • Reading about and taking notes on the ozone layer • Writing a reaction • Researching substitutes for CFCs • Debating the issue of the use of CFCs
5 Energy Needs Versus Alaskan Environment	• Reading about and discussing oil spills • Reading about and taking notes on oil spills • Writing an opinion letter to a corporation • Role playing

Unit 2: Air, Land, and Water (continued)

Segment & Topic	Functions in Postviewing Tasks
6 Ocean Plastic Pollution	• Reading about and discussing ocean plastic pollution • Researching ocean pollution • Writing a reaction • Conducting a poll about the problem of ocean plastic pollution • Brainstorming strategies for eliminating pollution

Unit 3: Energy, Resources, and Recycling

Segment & Topic	Functions in Postviewing Tasks
7 Earth Summit Snag	• Discussing the problems of developing countries • Reading about and taking notes on China's overpopulation • Writing a reaction • Researching countries with environmental problems • Brainstorming ways to help developing countries
8 Scientists Seek Proof Positive of Global Warming Effects	• Reading about and taking notes on the causes and effects of global warming • Conducting a poll about global warming • Researching substitutes for fossil fuels • Debating the issue of the government's role in preventing global warming
9 Recycling and Other Solutions to the Trash Problem	• Reading about and discussing recycling • Role playing • Researching recyclable packaging • Making a recycling map

Unit 4: Ideas and Applications

Segment & Topic	Functions in Postviewing Tasks
10 Solar Energy	• Discussing solar-powered cars • Reading about and taking notes on solar cooking and solar homes • Role playing • Writing a newspaper article • Conducting a survey about solar energy
11 A Look at European Mass Transit	• Discussing mass transit • Reading about and taking notes on the Maglev • Identifying factual errors • Role playing • Writing a letter to a politician
12 Environmental Concerns Cause Shopper Discretion	• Reading about and discussing food packaging • Researching food packaging • Conducting a survey on consumer habits

Suggestions for Self-Study

Although best used in a classroom setting with a teacher facilitating your progress, *Focus on the Environment* can also be used for self-study. Here are some suggestions to help you work through the material on your own.

- The exercises in the book—particularly those in the Previewing, Global Viewing and Intensive Viewing sections—are intended to help you gain a detailed understanding of the video segment. Because the video segments are interesting in themselves, you may be tempted to watch them without doing the exercises. Try to resist the temptation and to work systematically through the exercises for each video segment.

- Set realistic objectives for yourself as you work through the material. If, for example, one segment a week is too much, try working on one over two weeks. In any case, try to maintain a regular study schedule.

- Before beginning an exercise, read the directions carefully to make sure you know exactly what you are supposed to do.

- After you have finished each exercise, use the answer key in the Instructor's Manual to check your answers. Unless you are unable to provide your own answers, avoid looking at the answer key until you have completed the exercise, even if this means having to play the video, or a section of the video, a few more times.

- In cases where an exercise does not have clear-cut answers in the Instructor's Manual, you may find it simulating to work with another person: a native speaker or someone at your own level of competence in English.

- When you have completed the exercises for a video segment, you may find it satisfying to watch the entire video segment again to see how much better you understand it.

- Another useful option is to make use of the closed captions. If you have a decoder, you can follow along with the speakers and read the words on the screen. If you do not have a decoder, you can use the transcripts in the Instructor's Manual to reinforce and test your understanding of the videos.

Segment 1

Little Being Done To Stop Animal and Plant Extinction

From: *American Agenda*, 4/18/90
Runtime: 5:14
Begin: 00:36

Previewing

KEY QUESTIONS

1. What does the term *endangered species* mean?
2. What causes plant and animal species to become endangered?
3. What are some examples of plants and animals that are at risk?
4. What is being done to save endangered plants and animals? How successful are these efforts?

WHAT DO YOU ALREADY KNOW?

What do you already know about endangered plants and animals? Circle the letter of the answer you think is correct. (The answers are on page 2.)

1. When a species is labeled as *endangered*, what does it mean?
    a. The species is being killed at a faster rate than it can reproduce.
    b. The species cannot be successfully bred in the wild.
    c. The species cannot be successfully bred in zoos.
    d. The species has become rare in the wild and is in danger of disappearing completely.

2. What is the biggest single threat to most endangered animal species?
    a. Destruction of their natural environment.
    b. Illegal hunting.
    c. Other animals.
    d. Limited reproduction.

3. How many plants and animals become extinct every day?
   a. One.
   b. Two.
   c. Three.
   d. Four.

PREDICTION

Based on the title of the segment, *Little Being Done To Stop Animal and Plant Extinction*, and your own background knowledge, what information do you think will be included on the video?

1. _____

2. _____

3. _____

ESSENTIAL WORDS TO KNOW

The *italicized* words in each of the following sentences are used on the video. Read the sentences and suggest your own definition for each word.

1. Elephants are in danger of *extinction* due to hunting.

   extinction: _____

2. Governments are beginning to protect *threatened* animal species.

   threatened: _____

3. The natural *habitat* of the Siberian tiger is in southern and eastern Asia.

   habitat: _____

4. Some animal rights organizations would like all hunting to be *banned*.

   ban (v): _____

5. In the United States, it is illegal to spray *DDT* on plants.

   DDT: _____

6. Many animals do not breed when they are in *captivity*.

   captivity: _____

Global Viewing

GETTING THE MAIN IDEAS

Read the following sentences. Then watch the entire video segment and check (✓) the sentences that are true. Compare your answers with those of another student. If you disagree, watch the video again.

00:50-
05:35

_____ 1. People are more worried about the environment today than they were twenty years ago.
_____ 2. People now realize that only certain parts of the world are at risk.
_____ 3. Development is a major cause of animal extinction.
_____ 4. The Endangered Species Act has managed to save some animal species from extinction.
_____ 5. The United States Government has stopped adding animals to its list of threatened and endangered species.
_____ 6. Extinctions are occurring more rapidly now than they did in early human history.

Intensive Viewing

LISTENING CLOZE

The passage below is near the beginning of the video. Watch this part of the video again and fill in the blanks with the missing words.

01:13-
01:50

Barry Serafin: In the conflict between man and plants and animals,

_____ and _____ are still losing. A "For Sale" sign on a

patch of desert outside Tucson, Arizona means _____

is on the way and animals are on their way out. Throughout much of

the Southwest, the desert tortoise was recently added to the federal

government's list of _____ species. But it is not yet

_____ here in the Sonoran Desert. So when developers

move in, so does Candy Grunewald. With state permission, she relocates

the tortoises, placing them in _____ and _____—saving

their lives, but ending their days in the _____ .

CLASSIFYING ENDANGERED SPECIES

01:25-
04:18

Each of the endangered species below is shown on the video. To which class of animals does each species belong? Watch the video again and check (✓) the appropriate column.

	Fish	Reptiles	Mammals	Birds
1. desert tortoise	_____	_____	_____	_____
2. nene	_____	_____	_____	_____
3. bald eagle	_____	_____	_____	_____
4. red wolf	_____	_____	_____	_____
5. condor	_____	_____	_____	_____
6. black-footed ferret	_____	_____	_____	_____
7. snail darter	_____	_____	_____	_____
8. spotted owl	_____	_____	_____	_____

GETTING THE FIGURES

02:00-
03:52

Watch the video again. As you watch, fill in the notetaking form with the correct numbers.

I. Endangered Plants and Animals in Hawaii:

    A. Percent of rare and endangered U. S. birds and plants: _____

    B. Number of Hawaiian bird species already extinct: _____

    C. Number of nenes left in the wild: _____

    D. Number of acres of Hawaiian rain forest already destroyed: _____

II. Endangered Plants and Animals in other parts of the United States:

    A. Number of condors in captivity: _____

    B. Number of black-footed ferrets in captivity: _____

    C. Number of species on the Endangered Species List: _____

    D. Number of species that may also qualify for the list: _____

    E. Number of species added to the list each year: _____

GETTING THE FACTS

01:13-
03:52

Read the questions below. Then watch the video again and circle the best answer to each question.

1. What is the main cause of tortoise extinction in the Sonoran Desert?

    a. Illegal hunting and trapping.

    b. Development.

    c. Acid rain.

    d. Water pollution.

2. Where does Cindy Grunewald place the desert tortoises that she relocates?
   a. In other deserts.
   b. In rain forests.
   c. In sugarcane fields.
   d. In homes and museums.

3. How many of Hawaii's 140 bird species are endangered?
   a. None.
   b. One-third.
   c. One-half.
   d. All.

4. Why is it important to save native plant species in the Hawaiian rain forest?
   a. They may help to fight cancer and other diseases.
   b. They prevent water pollution.
   c. They produce bananas.
   d. They produce sugarcane.

5. What three bird populations have increased as a result of banning DDT?
   a. Bald eagles, nenes, and ospreys.
   b. Nenes, peregrine falcons, and ospreys.
   c. Nenes, condors, and bald eagles.
   d. Bald eagles, peregrine falcons, and ospreys.

6. Which North American species has been successfully reintroduced into the wild?
   a. The red wolf.
   b. The tortoise.
   c. The black-footed ferret.
   d. The spotted owl.

7. Which two endangered species are kept alive only in captivity?
   a. Bald eagles and ospreys.
   b. Peregrine falcons and red wolves.
   c. Condors and black-footed ferrets.
   d. Bald eagles and condors.

8. Which of the following is NOT given as a reason that the U.S. government adds only 50 to 60 species to the Endangered Species List each year?
   a. Limited manpower.
   b. Limited budgets.
   c. Lack of political will.
   d. Lack of threatened species.

TRUE OR FALSE?

Read the sentences below. Then watch the last part of the video. As you watch, decide whether each statement is true or false. Write *T* or *F*.

_____ 1. A small fish called the snail darter temporarily blocked construction of a dam in the 1970s.

_____ 2. Listing the spotted owl as an endangered species could mean the loss of jobs in the logging industry.

_____ 3. Frog populations in the United States and around the world are increasing rapidly.

_____ 4. Scientists think acid rain is a possible cause of the change in frog populations.

Language Focus

VOCABULARY CHECK

The sentences below are from the video segment. Match the *italicized* words and expressions with their equivalents from the list.

a. planned or designated
b. frightening sign
c. increased the speed of

d. things noticed or understood
e. become four times as great
f. consequences

_____ 1. In the twenty years between the first Earth Day and Earth Day this Sunday, that is the biggest change in *perceptions* about the environment.

_____ 2. They know that this is *slated* for development and they can't really do anything about it.

_____ 3. Banning the use of DDT . . . has helped to more than *quadruple* the number of bald eagles.

_____ 4. Banning the use of DDT . . . has *spurred* the recovery of peregrine falcons, ospreys, and other species.

_____ 5. These decisions involving the Endangered Species Act often have great *ramifications*, politically, economically, and socially.

_____ 6. Scientists say that frog deaths are a *chilling symptom* of something gone wrong in our global environment.

WORD FORMS

Choose the correct word form to complete each sentence.

1. *realization*   *realize*

   a. People are beginning to _____ that the earth is at risk.

   b. This _____ could cause people to take steps to save plant and animal life.

6

2. *extinction*   *extinct*
   a. Giant pandas are in danger of becoming _____ .
   b. The video is concerned with the subject of animal and plant

   _____ .

Postviewing

WHAT DO YOU THINK?

Write your answers to the following questions. Then discuss your answers with the class.

1. What have you learned from this video?

   _____

   _____

2. Do you think that protecting animal and plant species is necessary and important? Why or why not?

   _____

   _____

3. Are there any national protected areas in your home country? If so, where are they located? Describe which ones, if any, you have visited.

   _____

   _____

4. Can you think of any endangered species besides those mentioned on the video? If so, what are they? What is their habitat? Is there hope that their numbers will increase?

   _____

   _____

5. In your opinion, should all endangered species be preserved, or only certain ones? Explain your answer.

   _____

   _____

6. Based on the information on the video, do you think the list of endangered species will decrease, stay the same, or continue to grow? Give reasons for your answer.

   _____

   _____

READING FOR INSIGHT

Read the following article, and then fill in the outline that follows.

HABITATS AND WILDLIFE AT RISK

Loss of habitat is the principal threat to the survival of endangered plants and animals. Large areas of important natural habitat have already been lost, including 70% of the forests in Greece, 91% of the moist forests in Sudan, and nearly 100% of the tall grass prairie in the United States.

Population growth, agricultural expansion, the raising of cattle and other livestock, the building of cities and roads, and pollution are among the many causes of habitat destruction. While most countries recognize the need to protect natural habitats, few agree on how far that protection should extend. "National Protected Systems" make up 3.7% of the Earth's land area, but the amount of land protected in each country varies from a high of 38% in Ecuador to less than1% in countries such as Algeria, Nicaragua and Turkey. Both the number and size of "International Protection Systems" have increased over the years, but legal protection does not guarantee actual protection of the land. Economic and political factors often limit the amount of enforcement possible. Even in cases where an area itself is actually protected, activities outside its boundaries can severely affect the land and the wildlife that inhabits it.

Information about wildlife at risk in some countries is not always available. For instance, little is known about non-mammals in Africa and about Asian species in general. For some countries, however, information is readily available. For example 43 (13.4%) of the 320 mammalian species in Australia, and 123 (12.8%) of the 961 bird species in Mexico are at risk. Of the 46 different reptile species native to Puerto Rico, 15 (32.6%) are in jeopardy, and of the 29 amphibian species in France, 18 (62.1%) are threatened with extinction. As information becomes available, it is clear that the numbers of known and threatened species represent merely a fraction of those that actually exist.

Trade in animals and animal products can have disastrous effects on wildlife populations. Some bird species, such as the hyacinthine macaw of Brazil, have become endangered solely from being hunted for the pet trade. Much of the trade in animals and animal products is illegal. Many rare birds, such as the Tahiti lorikeet of French Polynesia are taken illegally from their habitat, and the ivory trade has reduced the total elephant population in Africa from an estimated 1,300,000 in 1979 to fewer than 650,000 today.

I. Habitats
    A. Some Countries Where Habitats Have Been Destroyed:

Country	Habitat Type	Percent Lost
1. _____	_____	_____
2. _____	_____	_____
3. _____	_____	_____

B. Some Causes of Habitat Destruction:

1. _____

2. _____

3. _____

4. _____

5. _____

C. National Protection Systems:

1. Percent of the earth's land in National Protection Systems: _____

2. Country with the largest percent of protected land: _____

3. Some countries with less than 1 percent of protected land:

   a. _____

   b. _____

   c. _____

II. Wildlife

A. Some Countries Where Wildlife is at Risk:

Country	Class of Animals (mammals, birds, etc.)	Number of Species Known	Number Threatened
1. _____	_____	_____	_____
2. _____	_____	_____	_____
3. _____	_____	_____	_____
4. _____	_____	_____	_____

B. Some Species Endangered by Trade in Animals and Animal Products:

1. _____

2. _____

3. _____

VISUALIZING THE DATA

Use the data in the article below to complete the pie chart that follows. Fill in the names of the countries and the percentage of ivory each country imported.

IVORY TRADE BANNED

In October of 1989, the Convention on International Trade in Endangered Species (CITES) moved the African elephant from Appendix II of CITES, which allows limited trade, to Appendix I, which bans all trade completely.

The decline in elephant populations—from 1.3 million in 1979 to 625,000 in 1989—prompted a majority of the world's nations to support the banning on all ivory trade. African nations showing the greatest change in elephant populations in the years between 1981 and 1989 include Sudan (down from 120,000 to 45,000), Tanzania (down from over 300,000 to fewer than 100,000), Zaire (down from 380,000 to fewer than 100,000), and Zambia (down from 150,000 to 50,000).

Support for the ban accelerated in the months before the CITES meeting. In June of 1989, Britain banned all ivory imports, both raw and worked, and Dubai announced a similar ban. The major importers of ivory in 1989 were Hong Kong (41%), Japan (24%), China (12%), Belgium (9%) and Singapore (4%). A variety of other nations consumed the remaining 10% of the world's ivory.

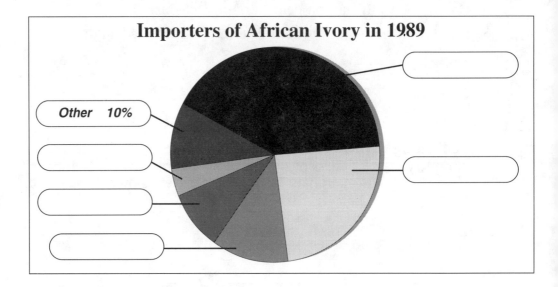

Importers of African Ivory in 1989

Other   10%

DEBATE

Divide the class into two teams: Team A and Team B. Conduct a debate on the banning of the ivory trade. In your team, do the following:

1. Read the background description for your side. Do NOT read the background description for the other team.
2. Prepare your arguments for the debate.
3. Before the debate begins, select a moderator to lead the discussion. Follow the procedure below when conducting the debate:
    A. Team A begins with a three-minute presentation.
    B. Team B then gives a three-minute presentation.
    C. Team A gives a three-minute response to Team B's presentation.
    D. Team B gives a three-minute response to Team A's presentation.
    E. The moderator evaluates the strengths of both arguments.

TEAM A

You will argue in favor of continued ivory trading. You believe that the ban will increase the price of ivory, which would make poaching (illegal hunting) more profitable and increase the risk of elephant poaching. You also believe that the ban will force the ivory trade further underground, making police detection more difficult.

TEAM B

You will argue in favor of banning ivory trading. You believe that the ban will increase efforts to control poaching and force countries that still continue to import ivory to shut off imports. You also believe that the ban will help persuade people not to buy ivory and encourage them to look for ivory substitutes.

MINI-SURVEY

Interview ten people. Ask them to identify five threatened or endangered animal species. Then ask them to specify what action, if any, they think should be taken to save animal populations. Was there any consistency among the answers? Summarize your findings in a one-page written report. Be prepared to read your report to the class.

WRITE A REACTION

Write your reaction (one-page maximum) to the following quotation:

"The deer, the horse, the great eagle, these are our brothers. . . the earth is our mother. . . all things are connected like the blood which unites one family. . ."

> Chief Seattle
> Letter to U.S. President Franklin Pierce, 1854

FINAL TASK: VALUES CLARIFICATION

Work in groups of five or six students. You are members of a team that is working to save the 10 endangered species listed below. You only have enough money and materials to work with one species at a time. Your task is to number the animals in the order you will try to save them, from 1 (the most important species) to 10 (the least important species). Use magazines, books and newspapers to get the information you will need to make your decision. Try to reach a group consensus on how the animals should be ranked. When you're done, present your group's final rankings to the class.

_____ Kemp's ridley turtle

_____ Queen Alexandra's birdwing butterfly

_____ Humpback whale

_____ Giant panda

_____ Golden toad

_____ Black lion tamarin

_____ Spanish lynx

_____ Black rhinoceros

_____ Aye-aye

_____ Asiatic lion

Segment 2

Medicines of the Rain Forests Disappearing

from: *The Health Show*, 1/7/90
Runtime: 5:52
Begin: 5:58

Note: This segment is not closed-captioned.

Previewing

KEY QUESTIONS

1. Where are most of the world's rain forests located?
2. What kinds of plants are found in rain forests?
3. Why are rain forests valuable?
4. Why are rain forests disappearing?

WHAT DO YOU ALREADY KNOW?

The topic of the video segment is rain forests. Write down your answers to the following questions. Then compare your answers with those of another student.

1. What do you already know about rain forests?

   _____

   _____

2. What are you unsure of about rain forests?

   _____

   _____

3. What do you hope to learn about rain forests?

   _____

   _____

ESSENTIAL WORDS TO KNOW

The *italicized* words in the sentences below are used in the video. Read the sentences and then match the words with their meanings.

pharmaceutical: She's a chemist for a large *pharmaceutical* company.
cultivate: Coffee is *cultivated* in the mountains of Colombia.
leukemia: The child died of *leukemia*.
extract (n):   The baker flavored the cake with lemon *extract*.
ethnobotanist: The *ethnobotanist* examined the leaf carefully.
apprentice: He was an *apprentice* to an electrician.

_____ 1. pharmaceutical
_____ 2. cultivate
_____ 3. leukemia
_____ 4. extract
_____ 5. ethnobotanist
_____ 6. apprentice

a. life-threatening disease of the blood
b. scientist who learns about plants in their natural habitats
c. connected with the making of medicine
d. person who is learning a trade, job, etc.
e. substance taken out by pressing, boiling, etc.
f. to plant, grow, and raise

Global Viewing

06:30-
08:12

SOUND OFF

Watch this part of the news story with the sound turned off. Then answer the following questions. When you finish answering the questions, compare your answers with those of another student.

1. What two things are happening to the forests and trees shown at the very beginning of the news story?

_____

_____

2. What organization does Dr. Gordon Cragg work for?

_____

_____

3. What is the connection between the pink flower shown on the video and the man working in the laboratory?

_____

_____

4. What do you think Dr. Gordon Cragg is saying?

_____

_____

CHECKING YOUR ANSWERS

Watch this part of the news story with the sound turned on. Compare your guesses in the Sound Off exercise with what you hear on the soundtrack.

06:30-
08:12

GETTING THE GENERAL IDEA

Watch the entire video segment. Then write brief answers to the questions below. When you finish, compare your answers with another student. If you disagree, watch the video again.

06:26-
10:36

1. Why are rain forests valuable?

   _____

   _____

2. Why are rain forests disappearing?

   _____

   _____

3. What kinds of information do ethnobotanists get from traditional healers?

   _____

   _____

Intensive Viewing

LISTENING CLOZE

The passage below is from the beginning of the video segment. Watch this part of the video segment again and fill in the blanks with the missing words.

06:26-
07:05

Karen Stone: For centuries now, people have relied on the _____ medicines of the _____ world to cure all kinds of illnesses. But soon this may no longer be possible. _____ which house these plants are fast becoming _____ , and as the _____ die, so possibly do we. Roger Caras reports.

Roger Caras: In the time it takes to deliver this report, about a half a square mile of _____ forest will be destroyed. Among the trees and smaller plants that may be _____ could be the cure for _____ , any number of _____ and other deadly and crippling _____ .

15

GETTING THE FACTS

Read the questions below. Then watch the video again and circle the best answer to each question.

1. By the time Roger Caras finishes his report, how much of the rain forest will be destroyed?
    a. A square mile.
    b. A quarter of a mile.
    c. Half of a square mile.
    d. Three quarters of a square mile.

2. What percentage of commonly used drugs comes from plant material?
    a. Ten percent.
    b. Twenty percent.
    c. Thirty percent.
    d. Forty percent.

3. How many of the world's plants have been evaluated for their pharmaceutical potential?
    a. Between one and five percent.
    b. Between five and ten percent.
    c. Between ten and fifteen percent.
    d. Between fifteen and twenty percent.

4. Which one of the following statements about the rosy periwinkle is TRUE?
    a. It is extinct.
    b. It is used to fight leukemia.
    c. It causes death in children.
    d. It is a large plant.

5. Twenty years ago, what was the death rate for children with leukemia?
    a. Twenty percent.
    b. Forty percent.
    c. Sixty percent.
    d. Eighty percent.

6. What is the survival rate for children with leukemia now?
    a. Fifteen percent.
    b. Twenty-five percent.
    c. Eighty-five percent.
    d. One hundred percent.

7. According to the video, how long will it be before most of the tropical rain forests disappear?
   a. Ten years.
   b. Twenty years.
   c. Thirty years.
   d. Forty years.

8. At what rate are plant species in the rain forests disappearing?
   a. One species a day.
   b. One species a week.
   c. One species a month.
   d. One species a year.

9. Who has examined many of the trees and bushes in the tropical rain forest in Belize for their pharmaceutical potential?
   a. The local people.
   b. Foreign pharmaceutical companies.
   c. Sugar cane companies.
   d. No one.

10. What is scheduled to happen to the Belizian rain forest shown on the video?
    a. It's going to be preserved by the local people.
    b. It's going to be replaced by a housing development.
    c. It's going to be purchased by a pharmaceutical company.
    d. It's going to be replaced by a sugar cane field.

11. What is Andrew Rancheron's occupation?
    a. He's an ethnobotanist.
    b. He's a traditional healer.
    c. He's a sugar cane farmer.
    d. He's a chemist.

12. Who is interested in Andrew Rancheron's work?
    a. His apprentices.
    b. His children.
    c. His grandchildren.
    d. Ethnobotanists.

Language Focus

WORD FORMS

The sentences below are from the video segment. The words in italics are either nouns, verbs, or adjectives. Complete the grid below by adding the other forms of the *italicized* word. In some categories, there is more than one possibility. Use a dictionary, if necessary. The first one has been done for you. When you finish, compare your chart with that of another student.

1. For centuries now, people have *relied* on the natural medicines of the plant world to cure all kind of illnesses.
2. Among the trees and smaller plants that may be exterminated could be the cure for AIDS, any number of cancers, and other *deadly* and crippling diseases.
3. Yet, only between one and five percent of the world's plants have been *evaluated* for their pharmaceutical potential.
4. At the National Cancer Institute, a new program has been launched to test substances, including plants, from all over the world for their possible *use*, including cancer and AIDS.
5. Around here are about 200 species of trees and bushes, only a small fraction of which have ever been examined for their pharmaceutical potential, except, of course, by the *local* people, who use many of them for medicines.
6. As we find through the *quantitative* ethnobotanical method, this forest is very valuable.
7. The amount of resources that we have in order to do this kind of work is relatively small in *comparison* to the forest.
8. We should really double or triple our effort, but that would only come with *additional* resources.

NOUN	VERB	ADJECTIVE
1. _____	relied	_____
2. _____	_____	deadly
3. _____	evaluated	_____
4. use	_____	_____
5. _____	_____	local
6. _____	_____	quantitative
7. comparison	_____	_____
8. _____	_____	additional

Postviewing

Write down your answers to the following questions. Then discuss your answers with other students.

1. What have you learned from this video?

   _____

   _____

2. In the U.S., the government pays farmers not to plant certain crops. Do you think the Belizian government of Belize should pay Garfield Rancheron not to cut down his trees and plant sugar cane? Why or why not?

   _____

   _____

3. Do rain forests exist in your home country? If so, are they coming down, or are efforts being made to save them?

   _____

   _____

4. Have you ever visited a rain forest? If so, where was it? Describe it to the class.

   _____

   _____

5. Would you like to be an ethnobotanist? Why or why not?

   _____

   _____

RELATED READING: QUIZ YOURSELF

What else do you know about rain forests? Take the following quiz and find out. (The answers are on page 20.)

QUIZ: Some More Facts About Rain Forests

1. All rain forests are located in hot, tropical areas. True or False? _____
2. Which three countries contain the world's largest remaining rain forests?
   a. Brazil, Indonesia and Zaire   b. Brazil, Canada and the United States
   c. Brazil, Mexico and Panama   d. Australia, Brazil and Russia

3. How many people live in the world's rain forests?
   a. 14 thousand   b. 14 million
   c. 140 thousand   d. 140 million

4. At what rate are the world's rain forests disappearing?
   a. 100 acres a day   b. 100 acres an hour
   c. 100 acres a minute   d. 100 acres a second

5. What percentage of the world's plant and animal species exist only in rain forests?
   a. 5 percent   b. 15 percent
   c. 35 percent   d. 50 percent

6. At least how many species of insects live in rain forests?
   a. 10 million   b. 20 million
   c. 30 million   d. 40 million

7. Which of these woods does not come from a rain forest?
   a. mahogany   b. black walnut
   c. teak   d. rosewood

8. Which of these animals does not live in a rain forest?
   a. llama   b. gorilla
   c. howler monkey   d. mouse deer

WRITE A BIOGRAPHY

Write a brief (one or two pages) imaginary biography of Andrew Rancheron, the 84-year-old traditional healer shown in the video sequence. Use your own imagination as well as information presented on the video itself. You may wish to use the questions below as a starting point. When your biography is complete, work in small groups and read your profile to the group.

1. When and where was Andrew Rancheron born?
2. What were his parents like?
3. Where does he work, and what exactly does he do?
4. How does he feel about his work?
5. What have been some significant events in his personal life?
6. What is his present situation, and how does he feel about it?

READING FOR INSIGHT

The value of tropical rain forests goes beyond medicine. Read the article, *Why Save Tropical Rain Forests*, to find out some other benefits to be gained from saving rain forests. Your task is to (1) read the comprehension and opinion questions that follow to guide your reading, and (2) discuss your answers to the questions with other students.

Why Save Tropical Rain Forests?

Tropical rain forests—those steamy jungles shown in movies, where it's always hot and it rains every day—are in trouble, and people around the world are becoming concerned. The rock star Sting has organized concerts to save the Brazilian rain forest, and dozens of environmental groups have raised millions of dollars to save tropical rain forests and send experts to help. Yet there are many people who say, "Why save rain forests? Aren't people more important than trees?"

Located in a belt of 33 countries, mostly around the equator, more than half of the tropical rain forests have disappeared in the past fifty years. Some are actually turning into deserts. With these forests disappearing at a rate of 100 acres per minute every minute, nearly everyone in the world has something to gain from saving them. For example, scientists have learned that over 1,300 rain forest plants in the Amazon have medicinal value. So far less than 10 percent of the plant and animal species in the world's rain forests have been studied for their possible medical benefits, and—of those that have been studied—less than one percent have been tested for the potential value in the treatment of cancer.

But the value of tropical rain forests goes beyond medicine. These forests have a critical impact on global weather patterns. Their vegetation absorbs enormous quantities of solar energy, thus affecting wind and rainfall patterns around the world. This vegetation contains huge amounts of carbon dioxide. As the forests disappear, the carbon dioxide is released into the air and contributes to "global warming"—what we know as the "greenhouse effect." Rain forests also help to prevent soil erosion in areas that could be damaged by floods and wind, and they also prevent pollution.

However, the benefits of rain forests are often overlooked, especially in developing countries where poor farmers move into forest land because they have no alternatives. Many governments encourage forest clearing to make room for mining, cattle, or export crops. The cutting down of forests is viewed in terms of a short term gain that benefits relatively few people—those who take over the land.

The loss of a tropical rain forest affects many more people—the forest people who lose their homes, the farmers whose soil erodes, the people whose water supplies are polluted, and others. Income from mining, export crops, timber, and cattle can be calculated in dollars, but the benefits of the forest as a protector of the land cannot.

COMPREHENSION QUESTIONS

1. Where are most of the world's tropical rain forests located?

_____

_____

2. How many tropical rain forests have disappeared in the past fifty years?

   _____

   _____

3. Besides medicine, what are some other benefits to be gained from saving rain forests?

   _____

   _____

4. Why are the benefits of rain forests often overlooked?

   _____

   _____

5. Who is affected by the loss of tropical rain forests?

   _____

   _____

IN YOUR OPINION

1. Do you believe that saving the rain forests is necessary and important? Why or why not?

   _____

   _____

2. What efforts, if any, do you think should be made to save the world's rain forests?

   _____

   _____

CONDUCT A POLL

Poll eight to ten people to find out their answers to the following question:

Are you concerned about the world's rain forests being cut down? Why or why not?

Keep a record of people's responses and note down any interesting comments they make. Tally the responses and summarize your findings in a one-page report. Be sure to include any interesting comments made by the people you interviewed.

REACHING A CONSENSUS

In groups of four or five, decide which of the statements given below best describes your collective viewpoint. After you reach a consensus, develop arguments in support of your group's position. Then present your group's conclusions to the class. Be prepared to defend your opinions to the entire class.

1. Garfield Rancheron should cut down his rain forest and plant sugar cane so that he can support his family.
2. The government of Belize should pay Garfield Rancheron enough money so that he can support his family without having to cut down his rain forest.
3. Pharmaceutical companies who wish to develop medicines from the plants on his property should pay Garfield Rancheron enough money so that he can support his family without having to cut down his rain forest.

FINAL TASK: VALUES CLARIFICATION

The list below presents some of the reasons people have given for saving rain forests. First rank the reasons from 1 (most important) to 10 (least important). Then work with five or six students and try to reach a group consensus on how the statements should be ranked. Present your group's final rankings to the class.

_____ To preserve knowledge. (As native rain forest people die or are forced to move, their knowledge of rain forest plants, animals and cycles is lost forever.)

_____ To prevent local problems. (The destruction of rain forests causes serious local problems such as soil erosion and water pollution.)

_____ To respect nature. (People have no right to destroy the world's rain forests and other habitats for their own purposes.)

_____ To preserve inspirational sources. (Tropical rain forests are unique, exotic places that have inspired the work of artists, writers, and others.)

_____ To save bird species outside the tropics. (Many bird species from other parts of the world, e.g. North American songbirds, migrate to tropical rain forests and depend on these forests for survival.)

_____ To keep the climate in balance. (Destroying tropical rain forests would drastically change weather patterns around the world.)

_____ To preserve cultural traditions. (Destroying rain forests destroys the cultural traditions of the native peoples who live in them.)

_____ To preserve tropical plant and animal species. (Destroying tropical rain forests would cause many tropical plant and animal species to be lost forever.)

_____ To allow new medicines to be discovered. (Unstudied plant and animal species in the rain forest could provide new medicines, including cancer cures.)

_____ To prevent wood and food products from becoming scarce. (People all over the world depend on rain forest products and foods, such as mahogany, bamboo, teak, bananas, nuts, and coffee.)

Segment 3

Marjory Douglas, 98-Year-Old Environmentalist

from: *World News Tonight*, 1/13/89
Runtime: 5:27
Begin: 11:12

Previewing

KEY QUESTIONS

1. What motivates a person to become an environmental activist?
2. What can one individual do to convince others to help save the environment?
3. What are the key personal characteristics of a successful environmental activist?

DISCUSSION

1. If you live to be over ninety, how do you think you will be spending your time when you reach that age?

   _____

   _____

2. How do you think the woman in the picture above spends her time?

   _____

   _____

PREDICTION

Based on the title of the segment, *Marjory Douglas, 98-Year-Old Environmentalist,* what information do you think will be included in the video segment?

1. _____

2. _____

3. _____

4. _____

ESSENTIAL WORDS TO KNOW

The following words are used on the video. Read the sentences. Then match the words with their meanings.

developer: *Developers* are interested in this property.

dredge: Engineers used machines to *dredge* the river.

grande dame: She is one of the *grande dames* of the environmental movement.

lecture circuit: After his book was published, he went on the *lecture circuit* across North America.

swamp: The hunter was lost in the *swamp*.

Yankee: He was surprised to hear himself called a *Yankee*.

_____ 1. developer   a. area of soft, wet land

_____ 2. dredge   b. great lady

_____ 3. grande dame   c. remove earth from the bottom of

_____ 4. lecture circuit   d. a person born in the northeastern

_____ 5. swamp   United States

_____ 6. Yankee   e. person who invests in new homes, buildings, etc. for a profit

                                   f. usual schedule of speeches and television appearances followed by notable speakers

Global Viewing

SOUND OFF

12:00-
14:00

The first part of the video shows pictures of Marjory Stoneman Douglas and the Florida Everglades. Watch the first part of the video with the sound turned off. Then answer the following questions:

1. What kind of person do you think Marjory Stoneman Douglas is?

_____

_____

2. What kind of place is the Florida Everglades?

_____

_____

3. What is the connection between Marjory Stoneman Douglas and the Everglades?

_____

_____

SOUND ON

Watch the first part of the video again, with the sound turned on. Compare your guesses in the Sound Off exercise with what you hear on the soundtrack.

12:00-
14:00

Intensive Viewing

LISTENING FOR DETAILS

Watch the first part of the video again and choose the best answer to each of the following questions.

11:30-
12:55

1. How long has Mrs. Douglas been working to save the Everglades?
   a. For 17 years.
   b. For 30 years.
   c. For 33 years.
   d. For 70 years.

2. What four things does Mrs. Douglas do as part of her work to save the Everglades?
   a. She lectures, makes television appearances, talks to politicians, and makes telephone calls.
   b. She reads, makes television appearances, talks to politicians, and makes telephone calls.
   c. She lectures, watches television, talks to politicians, and makes telephone calls.
   d. She lectures, makes television appearances, runs for political office, and makes telephone calls.

3. What reason does Mrs. Douglas NOT give to explain why she became involved with preserving the Everglades?

    a. They were there.

    b. Endangered animals lived there.

    c. Nobody else had done much about them.

    d. She learned they were very important.

TRUE OR FALSE?

Read the sentences below. Then listen to Peter Jennings, Charles Lee, and Joe Browder talk about Mrs. Douglas. Are the following statements true or false? Write *T* or *F*.

_____ 1. Peter Jennings says Mrs. Douglas opposed the idea of a conference on the future of the Everglades.

_____ 2. Charles Lee thinks Mrs. Douglas has had an important influence on public opinion.

_____ 3. Joe Browder thinks it is hard to believe what Mrs. Douglas says.

PUT THE EVENTS IN ORDER

Read the sentences below, which describe events in Marjory Douglas' life. Then watch the part of the video in which Peter Jennings and Mrs. Douglas talk about her life. As you watch, put the events into the correct order by numbering them from 1 to 7. The first event has been numbered for you.

_____ The Everglades National Park was established.

_____ She wrote a piece about the Everglades.

_____ She moved south and went to work for her father at the Miami Herald.

_1_ Marjory Douglas was born in Minneapolis and raised in New England.

_____ She became interested in setting up the Everglades National Park.

_____ *Ms. Magazine* made her one of its women of the year.

_____ She went to Wellesley College.

NOTETAKING

Read the following questions. Then watch the last part of the video and make brief notes on your answers. Compare your notes with those of another student. If you disagree, watch the video again.

1. When Mrs. Douglas is not working, how does she spend her time?

    _____

    _____

2. In what way is Mrs. Douglas physically handicapped?

   _____

   _____

3. How does Mrs. Douglas feel about being ninety-eight years old?

   _____

   _____

4. What adjectives does Peter Jennings use to describe Mrs. Douglas?

   _____

   _____

5. What does Mrs. Douglas say it is "more fun to fight for"?

   _____

   _____

6. What did the Army Corps of Engineers do to prevent the Kissimmee River from flooding?

   _____

   _____

LISTENING CLOZE

The passage below is from the last part of the video. Watch this part of the video again and fill in the blanks with the missing words.

15:05–16:25

Peter Jennings: Today, when she is not on the lecture circuit—in even

greater _____ because *Ms. Magazine* has just made her one of its

women of the year—she works at the small house she built in the 1920s in

Coconut Grove. There is always work to be done. Or a good book to be

_____ to now. Her partial blindness has not dulled her passion

for literature. And what a wonderful attitude she has about getting on a bit.

Marjory Stoneman Douglas: I'm glad to be 98. Better than being dead,

you know.

Peter Jennings: Independent, outspoken, dedicated, and still ready to

_____ ____ all comers.

Marjory Stoneman Douglas: Why not? It's a lot more fun to fight for

something important than to fight for something _____ ,

and it's a lot more fun to fight for something than not to fight

for _____ .

Peter Jennings: And so we choose Marjory Stoneman Douglas. And we do like her way with _____. When the Army Corps of Engineers took all the twists and _____ out of the Kissimmee River, so as to _____ flooding, the Corps said, Mrs. Douglas said she thought it was more likely the engineers' mothers had never let them play with mud pies. She was right about the river. A short while later, the State of Florida had to undo the _____ and start restoring the river to its natural course.

Language Focus

UNDERSTANDING COLLOQUIAL LANGUAGE

The sentences and phrases below are from the video. Match the *italicized* words and expressions with their equivalents from the list.

a. for the purpose of
b. be destroyed or ruined
c. resist all opponents
d. hidden facts or reasons for something
e. impossible
f. becoming older
g. contacts people by telephone
h. of first or highest importance
i. continues to do the same thing
j. forces (people) to listen

_____ 1. *Out of the question* for the woman we've chosen this week.
_____ 2. She is 98 and she *is still at it.*
_____ 3. Otherwise, the whole country will *go to the dickens.*
_____ 4. She . . . *bends* politicians' *arms* . . .
_____ 5. She . . . *works the phone* daily.
_____ 6. *All in the name of* preserving a wonder of nature.
_____ 7. I think there's a great body of water that *above everything* must be preserved.
_____ 8. Marjory Douglas sees a lot *more* here *than meets the eye.*
_____ 9. And what a wonderful attitude she has about *getting on a bit.*
_____ 10. Independent, outspoken, dedicated, and still ready to *take on all comers.*

PAST CONDITIONAL

Complete the sentences below with the correct tense of the verbs in parentheses. The first one is done for you.

1. If Marjory Stoneman Douglas (move, negative) <u>hadn't moved</u> to Florida in 1915, she (be, negative) <u>wouldn't have been</u> able to go to work for her father.

2. If her father (found, negative) _____ the Miami Herald, she (go) _____ to work for another newspaper.

3. If she (write, negative) _____ an article about the Everglades in 1922, she (become, negative) _____ interested in setting up the Everglades National Park.

4. The Conference on the Future of the Everglades (happen, negative) _____ if she (make, negative) _____ people aware of the importance of the area.

5. The public (realize, negative) _____ the importance of the Everglades if she (keep) _____ silent.

6. If she (work, negative) _____ to save the Everglades, developers (destroy) _____ the whole area.

7. If the Army Corps of Engineers (listen) _____ to Mrs. Douglas, they (cause, negative) _____ so much damage to the Kissimmee River.

8. If Marjory Douglas (fight, negative) _____ to save the Everglades, she (fight) _____ for some other important cause.

WORD FORMS

The sentences below are from the video segment. The words in italics are either nouns, verbs, or adjectives. Complete the grid that follows by adding the other forms of the *italicized* word. In some categories, there is more than one possibility. Use a dictionary, if necessary. When you finish, compare your chart with that of another student.

1. For most of us still working, it can be *comforting* every so often to dream of retirement, that is to say, the kind of retirement which is synonymous with relaxation.

2. A whole *generation* has come of age since then, and she is still working.

3. She lectures and makes television appearances and bends *politicians'* arms and works the phone daily.

4. We've got to realize what we've got and *preserve* it and that goes for the entire country.

5. It comes as no surprise to Floridians that a *conference* on the future of the Everglades, opening tonight in southern Florida, probably would not have happened without the efforts of Marjory Douglas.

6. It was a piece that she had written about the Everglades in 1920 that *accelerated* her interest in seeing that the waterway was not tampered with.

NOUN	VERB	ADJECTIVE
1. _____	comforting	_____
2. generation	_____	_____
3. politicians	_____	_____
4. _____	preserve	_____
5. conference	_____	_____
6. _____	accelerated	_____

Postviewing

WHAT DO YOU THINK?

Write your answers to the following questions. Then discuss your answers with the class.

1. Why do you think Mrs. Douglas has been successful in her efforts to save the Florida Everglades?

   _____

   _____

2. In your home culture, at what age do the majority of people retire? How do they spend their retirement?

   _____

   _____

3. Do you think more elderly people should follow Mrs. Douglas' example and work for environmental causes instead of relaxing in their retirement? Why or why not?

   _____

   _____

4. Do you know of elderly people in your home culture who are involved in environmental causes? If so, describe them and the causes they are involved in.

   _____

   _____

5. According to Mrs. Douglas, "the American tendency to use things up has got to stop." What does she mean by this? Can you give an example?

_____

_____

6. Would you be interested in meeting Marjory Stoneman Douglas? Why or why not?

_____

_____

READING FOR INSIGHT

The excerpt is from *Florida: The Long Frontier*, written by Marjory Stoneman Douglas in 1967. Read the questions that follow the article, and then read the excerpt to find the answers.

Florida: The Long Frontier

That same year of 1947 the Army Corps of Engineers, who had been called by the state to study and drain the Everglades, put their first plan to work. Today the unfinished plan has made the Everglades almost unrecognizable. And the Everglades National Park, set up by the federal government with the understanding that there would always be enough fresh water, which is its greatest necessity, has only been saved from drought and ruin by hurricane water and the forced opening of floodgates by the reluctant and uninterested Central and Southern Flood Control Board.

The 112-mile 36-foot Hoover Dam around Lake Okeechobee will be completed in 1969 at a cost of $100 million. The water level of the 750-square-mile lake will be raised to 2.5 feet, storing 30 billion gallons of water. The Caloosahatchee River, once widened will be widened again, by which fresh lake water can be dumped more quickly than ever into the sea. The Kissimmee River flow will be controlled by locks and dams and spillways. The St. Lucie Canal will continue to be used to dump floodwater into St. Lucie Inlet, where it so often kills off the salt-water fish. . . . Three conservancy areas in Palm Beach, Broward and Dade counties have been built to hold water for the east coast cities. They have been slow to fill because standing water evaporates. . . .

Perhaps it is not the Engineers' plan itself which brought the once-marvellous Everglades and park to the threat of doom so much as political pressure on some of the members of the Central and Southern Control District. Perhaps the plan can be improved. Certainly this Florida area contains the greatest natural force of fresh water that any state in the Union can boast. There would be water enough for vegetables, cities and the Everglades National Park if only it were intelligently and wisely managed.

This is one of the great continuing fights against the destruction of Florida's great resources, which is yet to be won. But the astonishing and heartening thing is the outpouring of support raised, from within the state and all over the country, against this waste and destruction. It is as if more and more people everywhere are learning what we must do to save our greatest heritages. In Florida, especially, the people are being called on to choose between a blind obedience to the sheer increasing pressure of populations and the vital necessity for building finer cities in a balanced and preserved natural background which alone can give them meaning and value. The future lies in them and in the strength with which man himself can set his powers of creation against his impulses for destruction.

Reprinted from *Florida: The Long Frontier*, by Marjory Stoneman Douglas, 1967, Harper & Row, pp. 282-283.

COMPREHENSION QUESTIONS

1. According to Mrs. Douglas, what two things saved the Everglades National Park from drought and ruin?

_____

_____

2. What were some specific, intended effects of the Army Engineers' plan?

_____

_____

3. In Mrs. Douglas' opinion, how will the fight to save the Everglades be won?

_____

_____

INTERPRETING THOUGHTS

Work in groups and discuss the following question:

What did Mrs. Douglas mean when she said she thought it "more likely the engineer's mothers had never let them play with mud pies"?

WRITE A REACTION

Write your reaction (one page maximum) to the following quotation:

"There are too many things in which to be interested, too many things to know about for anybody to be bored or unhappy."

Marjory Stoneman Douglas
Voice of the River

INTERVIEW TASK

Interview a person who is involved in environmental activities. You may wish to use the questions below to guide the interview. When you've finished, report the information to the class.

1. What environmental issues concern you most?
2. What sorts of environmental activities have you participated in?
3. How and when did you first become involved in environmental work?
4. What motivated you to become involved in environmental work?

MINI-RESEARCH TASK

Listed below are some well-known environmentalists, living and dead. Using magazines, books, or newspapers, find out who they are and write a sentence or two about each one. Also, write a summary sentence or two that describes what they all have in common.

1. Rachel Carson
2. Jacques Cousteau
3. Diane Fossey
4. John Muir
5. Pete Seeger

MAP READING

Using a map of the United States, find the national parks. Make a list of at least 15 parks and their locations. Compare your list to those of the other students. Did they locate any national parks that you did not?

SPECIAL WRITING ASSIGNMENT

Identify an area of your home country that you think deserves to be a national park. Write your reasons for your choice (one page maximum).

FINAL TASK: MAKE A SCHEDULE

Work in a group of four or five people. Together, make up an outline of what you think would be a typical week's schedule for Marjory Stoneman Douglas. Use your imagination. Be sure to include time spent on environmental activities such as lecturing, making television appearances, talking to politicians, and making telephone calls, as well as leisure activities. Then choose a member of your group to present your schedule to the class.

Segment 4

EPA Says Ozone Depletion More Serious Than Thought

from: *American Agenda,* 9/18/91
Runtime: 5:04
Begin: 16:43

Previewing

KEY QUESTIONS

1. What is the ozone layer? Why is it important to life?
2. What causes ozone loss?
3. What are some of the effects of ozone loss?
4. What is being done to prevent ozone loss?
5. What are some obstacles to reducing ozone loss?

PREDICTION

Read the news articles below. Then, based on the information in the articles, your own background knowledge, and the title of the segment, *EPA Says Ozone Depletion More Serious Than Thought,* predict the information you think will be included in the video.

British Scientists Find Hole in Ozone Layer

1985 - Dr. Joe Farman and his colleagues on the British Antarctic survey team report the discovery of a gigantic hole in the ozone layer, the protective shield of ozone gas (a type of oxygen) that keeps the sun's harmful rays from penetrating the earth's atmosphere. The hole is estimated to be larger than the continental United States and higher than Mount Everest.

Study Reveals CFCs Cause Ozone Damage

1987 - A study of the ozone hole over Antarctica reveals that chloroflourocarbons (CFCs)— chemicals commonly used in refrigerators, insulation, fast food packaging and aerosol sprays—are the main cause of ozone destruction.

1. _____

2. _____

3. _____

ESSENTIAL WORDS TO KNOW

The *italicized* words are all used on the video. Read the sentences and then match the words or expressions with their meanings below.

a. growths over the eyeball which can cause blindness

b. to release or discharge (liquid, smoke, etc.)

c. dangerous beams of light from the sun

d. great decrease

e. damage to the natural system which protects one from a disease

f. to move or put in place

_____ 1. Space shuttles are used to *deploy* satellites.

_____ 2. *Ultraviolet rays* cause sunburn and promote skin cancer.

_____ 3. The forest fire caused a *depletion* in the wildlife population.

_____ 4. His vision improved greatly when his *cataracts* were removed.

_____ 5. She was hospitalized because she had an *immune disorder*.

_____ 6. Automobile engines *vent* carbon monoxide into the air.

Global Viewing

GETTING THE MAIN IDEAS

Watch the video and choose the best answer to each question.

16:55-21:25

1. What do scientists say is happening to the ozone layer?
   a. They say it's getting bigger.
   b. They say it's being destroyed rapidly.
   c. They say it's moving closer to the earth.
   d. They say it's staying the same.

2. Why is the ozone layer important to life on Earth?
   a. It protects the earth from the ultraviolet rays of the sun.
   b. It keep the earth in orbit.
   c. It makes it possible to deploy satellites.
   d. All of the above.

3. What did the EPA (Environmental Protection Agency) report say about the ozone layer?
   a. It said the problem was really nothing to be concerned about.
   b. It said the problem had been eliminated.
   c. It said the problem had been slowed down by 90%.
   d. It said the problem was twice as bad as expected.

4. What is causing the depletion of the ozone layer?
    a. CFCs.
    b. The EPA.
    c. Satellites.
    d. All of the above.

5. Besides over the South Pole, where else has there been a loss of ozone?
    a. Over the United States.
    b. Over Western Europe.
    c. Over all of the developing countries.
    d. All of the above.

6. What is the biggest obstacle to reducing ozone depletion?
    a. Finding a replacement for CFCs.
    b. Servicing existing air conditioners and refrigerators.
    c. Getting local governments to cooperate.
    d. Finding a way to recycle CFCs.

Intensive Viewing

LISTENING CLOZE

The passage below is from the first part of the video. Watch this part of the video again and fill in the blanks with the missing words.

16:55-
18:16

Peter Jennings: Like the President, we've put the environment on the American Agenda tonight. When the space shuttle Discovery _____ at Edward's Air Force Base in California early this morning, it was completing a _____ to, among other things, deploy the first of a series of _____ designed to take a close look at the Earth's environment from 370 miles up. For at least the next two years, this first satellite will send back _____ on the ozone layer, which scientists say is being _____ away at an alarming rate. Our Agenda reporter is Ned Potter.

Ned Potter: Every astronaut who looks back from space marvels how delicate the _____ seems. Its ozone layer, for instance, is very _____ but absolutely critical. Without it, the sun's ultraviolet rays would make the Earth unlivable. Instruments on planes and satellites have already _____ the ozone shield is being thinned out, but the latest report from the Environmental Protection Agency had stunning news. The EPA, which _____ sounds alarmist, says the ozone problem is twice as bad as anyone expected.

William Reilly: Ozone depletion is in the top _____ of threats to health and the environment for the United States and the rest of the world.

Dr. Michael Oppenheimer: We should _____ as if the ozone depletion situation is an _____ . We should pull out all stops.

NOTETAKING

18:17-20:25

Watch the rest of the video segment and take brief notes on the answers to the questions below. Then compare your answers with those of another student. If you disagree, watch the video again.

1. What are some uses of CFCs?

   _____

   _____

2. What health problems are mentioned as possible consequences (results) of ozone depletion?

   _____

   _____

3. How many countries have already agreed to phase out CFCs, and by what deadline?

   _____

   _____

4. What is Elizabeth Cooke's opinion regarding the seriousness of the ozone problem?

   _____

   _____

5. According to Tony Vogelsberg, what is the problem with phasing out existing air conditioners and replacing them with machines that use alternative chemicals?

   _____

   _____

TRUE OR FALSE?

Read the sentences below. Then watch the last part of the video. As you watch, decide whether each statement is true or false. Write *T* or *F*.

20:25-
21:00

_____ 1. Most mechanics in Denver vent CFCs into the atmosphere.
_____ 2. Venting CFCs into the atmosphere is illegal in Denver.
_____ 3. Air conditioning repairmen use backpacks to collect CFCs.
_____ 4. Refrigerator repairmen in Denver carry ozone-saver bags.
_____ 5. CFCs cannot be recycled and sold.

Language Focus

GETTING THE MEANING FROM CONTEXT

Read the excerpts below. Then view the video again, paying special attention to the *italicized* words and expressions. Choose the best definition for each.

17:26-
19:40

Every astronaut who looks back from space *marvels* how *delicate* the atmosphere seems. Its ozone layer, for instance, is very thin but absolutely *critical*; without it, the sun's ultraviolet rays would make the earth unlivable.

1. *marvels*:
   a. is surprised or astonished (at)
   b. is bored (by)
   c. doubts
   d. is uncertain about

2. *delicate*:
   a. of thick, strong material
   b. of fine, thin material
   c. of dark-colored material
   d. of light-colored material

3. *critical*:
   a. easy to destroy
   b. hard to destroy
   c. important
   d. unimportant

Instruments on planes and satellites have already proved the ozone shield is being thinned out, but the latest report from the Environmental Protection Agency had *stunning* news. The EPA, which rarely sounds *alarmist,* says the ozone problem is twice as bad as anyone expected.

4. *stunning*:
   a. shocking
   b. calming
   c. boring
   d. cheerful

5. *alarmist*:
   a. disappointed
   b. hopeful
   c. like a person who expects danger, often without cause
   d. like a person who has already experienced danger

We should act as if the ozone depletion situation is an emergency. We should *pull out all stops.*

6. *pull out all stops*:
   a. stop working
   b. stop worrying
   c. do nothing to help a situation
   d. do everything possible to help a situation

It means getting rid of CFCs, the chemical *lifeblood* of car air conditioners and refrigerators, of foam *insulation* and computer factories.

7. *lifeblood*:
   a. waste product
   b. useless element
   c. something that gives strength and energy
   d. something that depletes strength and energy

8. *insulation*:
   a. heating material
   b. material to keep out heat or cold
   c. cooling material
   d. raw material

The biggest *obstacle* is finding a replacement to run air conditioners and refrigerators. That's *crucial* because they alone use almost half the world's CFCs.

9. *obstacle*:

    a. cost

    b. difficulty

    c. benefit

    d. evidence

10. *crucial*:

    a. of the greatest importance

    b. of the least importance

    c. expensive

    d. inexpensive

Postviewing

WHAT DO YOU THINK?

Write your answers to the following questions. Then discuss your answers with the class.

1. What have you learned from this video?

    _____

    _____

2. Many countries have agreed to phase out CFCs, but many developing countries—China, for example—have refused to sign the agreement. Why do you think this is so?

    _____

    _____

3. Based on the information on the video, do you think the threat to the ozone layer will increase, stay the same, or decrease? Give reasons for your answer.

    _____

    _____

Read the article below to learn more about: (1) the extent of ozone depletion around the world, and (2) the effects of ultraviolet radiation. Then fill in the outline that follows.

THE OZONE IS VANISHING

In 1974 California-based scientists F. Sherwood Rowland and Mario J. Molina discovered a link between CFCs and ozone depletion. According to their estimates, if CFC emissions continued at the 1974 rate (they are now much higher), up to 13% of the ozone layer would be destroyed by the end of the 21st century. Rowland and Molina had no idea that ozone loss would be particularly severe over Antarctica or over any other part of the world. Since the Rowland-Molina ozone alert, ground-based and satellite data have revealed a 50% ozone loss over Antarctica. Data analyzed in 1990 showed that ozone levels over the northern hemisphere had declined by up to 8% in the previous decade. However, more recent data reveals that during late winter and early spring, ozone levels above the northernmost regions of the U.S., Canada, Europe and Russia can be temporarily depleted by as much as 40%.

With less ozone in the atmosphere, increasing amounts of ultraviolet (UV) radiation reach the Earth's surface. This can have disastrous effects on human health. UV exposure affects the skin, causing premature aging, wrinkling, and various forms of skin cancer. UV rays can make the lens of the eye cloud up with cataracts, which, if untreated, can lead to blindness. Excess UV radiation may also affect human immune systems, making the body unable to fight off disease. But human life is not the only kind of life at risk from UV exposure. High doses of UV radiation can reduce the yield of basic food crops, such as soybeans, and UV-B, the most dangerous form of UV light, penetrates below the surface of the ocean. There it can kill the plankton (one-celled plants) and krill (tiny shrimplike animals) that serve as food for larger fish.

In the southern hemisphere, the impact of ozone loss is already being felt. Weather patterns have begun to change in Antarctica. In Australia, health officials have reported a threefold rise in skin cancer caused by excessive radiation. Australian scientists blame UV radiation for their country's lower yields of such food crops as peas, wheat, and other cereal plants. How long will it be before the more northern countries begin to show the effects of ozone destruction?

I. Discovery of the Link Between Ozone Depletion and CFCs

   A. Scientists who made the discovery:

      1. _____

      2. _____

   B. Year the discovery was made: _____

II. Data on Ozone Depletion
   A. Percent ozone loss over Antarctica: _____
   B. Percent ozone loss over the northern hemisphere: _____
   C. Percent ozone loss over the northernmost regions of the U.S., Canada, Europe, and Russia from late winter to early spring: _____
III. Potential Effects of UV Radiation
   A. How UV affects human health:
      1. Effects on skin:
         a. _____
         b. _____
         c. _____
      2. Effect on eyes: _____
      3. Effect on immune systems: _____
IV. Effects of Ozone Loss Already Felt
   A. In Antarctica: _____
   B. In Australia:
      1. Percent increase in skin cancer: _____
      2. Food crops affected:
         a. _____
         b. _____
         c. _____

RELATED READING: ELIMINATING CHLOROFLOUROCARBONS

Read the article below. Then answer the comprehension and opinion questions that follow and discuss your answers with another student.

WHO PAYS THE BILL?

The 1985 discovery of the hole in the ozone layer over Antarctica forced the leaders of industrialized nations to recognize that something needed to be done. The ozone layer had to be saved and the way to save the ozone layer was clear: eliminate the production and use of chloroflourocarbons (CFCs). However, this is easier said than done because the use of CFCs is widespread in almost every society of the world. Substitutes have been developed for CFCs, but they are expensive and can cause safety problems. In 1987, more than two dozen countries gathered in Montreal to sign a treaty known as the "Montreal Protocol." This agreement provided for a 50% phaseout of CFCs over the next ten years. To date, more than 60 other countries have also agreed to phase out CFCs.

However, if a worldwide ban is to be effective, it needs to have the cooperation of every present and potential user of CFCs. The fact is that many developing countries still have not signed the protocol. The richer, industrialized nations were quick to go along with the phaseout, but China, India and some other rapidly industrializing countries refused to sign the original agreement. They said they could not afford the high cost of substituting alternatives for CFCs. After a special $240 million fund, financed by the developed countries, was created to help developing nations switch to CFC-free technologies, China signed a revised version of the protocol in 1991. India has not yet signed the agreement.

In the view of the developing countries, ozone depletion is a problem created by the U.S., Western Europe and Japan. They feel the lifestyles of the people in their countries will be improved by allowing them to produce refrigerators, air conditioners and other ozone-depleting appliances. Why, they ask, should their citizens be denied the use of products already common in Western homes? And then there is the cost of changing technologies. The developing countries feel it is unfair to ask them to pay the cost—in both money and inconvenience—of the mistakes made by the richer, highly industrialized nations. What price is too high to protect the atmosphere shared by all the world's people? And who should pay the bill?

COMPREHENSION QUESTIONS

1. Why is it so difficult to eliminate the production and use of CFCs?

   _____

   _____

2. What is wrong with substitutes that have been developed for CFCs?

   _____

   _____

3. Who must cooperate if an international ban on CFCs is to be effective?

   _____

   _____

4. Why did China and India refuse to sign the original Montreal Protocol?

   _____

   _____

5. In the view of the developing countries, who is responsible for the depletion of the ozone layer?

   _____

   _____

IN YOUR OPINION

1. Governments in developing countries want the industrialized nations to give them money to use substitutes for CFCs. Do you agree with this idea? Explain your answer.

    _____

    _____

2. Are efforts being made to reduce the use and production of CFCs in your home country? If so, what is being done?

    _____

    _____

WRITE A REACTION

Write a one-page reaction to the quotation below.

"India recognizes the threat to the environment and the necessity for a global burden sharing to control it. But is it fair that the industrialized countries who are responsible for the ozone depletion should arm-twist the poorer nations into bearing the cost of their mistakes?"

Maneka Gandhi
Former Indian Minister of the Environment

MINI-RESEARCH TASK

Listed below are some substitutes for the CFCs used in aerosol sprays, refrigerators, air conditioners, cleaning agents, foam insulation and packing materials. Using magazines, books and newspapers, find out what products each substitute can be used for (aerosol sprays, refrigerators, etc.) as well as the advantages and disadvantages of the substitute. Write a one-page report summarizing the information you obtain.

1. HCFCs (hydrochloroflourocarbons)
2. HFCs (hydroflourocarbons)
3. Hydrocarbons (such as butane, propane)
4. Ammonia

FINAL TASK: DEBATE

Divide the class into two teams: Team A and Team B. Conduct a debate on the use of CFCs. In your team, do the following:

1. Read the background description for your side. Do NOT read the background description for the other team.
2. Prepare your arguments for the debate.
3. Before the debate begins, select a moderator to lead the discussion. Follow the procedure below when conducting the debate:
   A. Team A begins with a three minute presentation.
   B. Team B then gives a three-minute presentation.
   C. Team A gives a three-minute response to Team B's presentation.
   D. Team B gives a three-minute response to Team A's presentation.
   E. The moderator evaluates the strengths of both arguments.

TEAM A

You will take the view of the industrialized countries, that everyone should stop using CFCs. You believe that all the countries of the world should follow the example of the 90 countries who have already signed the Montreal Protocol and agreed to reduce their use of CFCs.

TEAM B

You will take the view of the developing countries who want a better standard of living at the lowest possible cost. You believe that the lifestyles of people in developing countries will be improved by allowing them to produce the refrigerators, air conditioners, etc. that are found in Western homes.

Segment 5

Energy Needs Versus Alaskan Environment

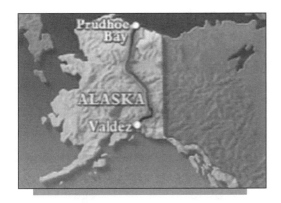

from: *American Agenda*, 3/30/89
Runtime: 5:39
Begin: 21:50

Note: This segment is not closed-captioned.

Previewing

KEY QUESTIONS

1. How can we balance the need for energy with the need to protect the environment?
2. Is drilling for oil in or near environmentally sound areas justified?
3. What is the oil industry's record with regard to shipping and drilling for oil?
4. Can oil companies be relied upon to police their own shipping and drilling practices with respect to the environmental impact of such activities?

PREDICTION

On March 24, 1989, the American oil tanker *Exxon Valdez* ran aground in Prince William Sound, Alaska, spilling more than 11 million gallons of oil that spread over 1,087 miles of beach. The video segment, *Energy Needs Versus the Alaskan Environment*, was broadcast six days after the accident. Based on your background knowledge of the *Exxon Valdez* oil spill—or of oil spills in general—what information do you think will be included in the video?

1. _____

2. _____

3. _____

ESSENTIAL WORDS TO KNOW

The following words are used on the video. Read the sentences below. Then match the words with their meanings.

violation: He was fined for a traffic *violation.*
potentially: This is a *potentially* dangerous situation.
corrode (v):   Acid will cause most metals to *corrode.*
tundra: The Alaskan *tundra* freezes in winter.
police (v):   United Nations forces *policed* the area.
slick (n):   An oil *slick* remains in the bay.

_____ 1. violation
_____ 2. potentially
_____ 3. corrode
_____ 4. tundra
_____ 5. police
_____ 6. slick

a. become worn or destroyed slowly (especially by chemical action)
b. enforce the laws
c. thick film covering the surface of the sea
d. act of breaking a law
e. wide, treeless plain of the arctic regions
f. possibly, but not yet actually

Global Viewing

22:03-
26:32

FIND THE MAIN IDEAS

Watch the video and choose the best answer to the following question:

1. Which reason is NOT given for continuing to drill for oil in Alaska?
   a. A large part of the Alaskan economy is based on oil.
   b. If we don't get oil from Alaska, we'll have to get it from someplace else.
   c. Most of the oil drilling in Alaska is done offshore.
   d. The oil industry's record in Alaska continues to improve.

22:03-
26:32

COMPREHENSION CHECK

Read the following sentences. Then watch the video again. As you watch, decide whether each statement is true or false. Write *T* or *F*.

_____ 1. Nancy Lethcoe feels that Prince William Sound has been destroyed.
_____ 2. Lisa Speer wants to see more oil development in Prince William Sound.
_____ 3. A large part of the Alaskan economy is based on oil development.
_____ 4. Frank Murkowski thinks we should look for oil somewhere other than Alaska.
_____ 5. Bill Stevens is critical of the oil industry's environmental record in Alaska.

_____ 6. Ann Strickland thinks oil companies have done a good job of policing themselves.

_____ 7. Athena Zecevic thinks people should be angry at the oil companies.

_____ 8. Gasoline prices in California have risen because of the *Exxon Valdez* oil spill.

Intensive Viewing

LISTENING CLOZE

22:03-
23:22

The passage below is from the first part of the video. Watch this part of the video again and fill in the blanks with the missing words.

Peter Jennings: We're going to go back up to Alaska for tonight's American Agenda. The oil spill in Prince William Sound has once again focused _____ on a very basic question: How do we balance the need for energy with the need to _____ the environment we live in? If you can _____ what it was like waiting on those long lines at the gas _____ ten years ago, if you can see and touch and smell the oil tonight in Valdez Harbor, you might _____ even more the dilemma and the debate. Here's Ned Potter.

Ned Potter: The oil from the Exxon Valdez has _____ the backyard of Jim and Nancy Lethcoe, literally. They live on this _____ in Valdez Harbor. They moved here from Wisconsin because they _____ Prince William Sound.

Nancy Lethcoe: We've just _____ one of the jewels of the United States if not the _____ , and we just can't go on ruining things.

Ned Potter: Go on ruining things. Is that what it means to _____ petroleum? The accident has sharpened the old argument between environment and energy in this _____ place.

Lisa Speer: You can't have an environmentally sound area and oil _____ . You have to choose between one or the other.

51

NOTETAKING

Watch the rest of the video and fill in the notetaking form below.

23:25-
26:32

1. Facts about the oil business in Alaska:
   a. percentage of the Alaskan economy based on oil: _____
   b. length of the Alaskan pipeline: _____
   c. source of the Alaskan pipeline: _____

2. Violations listed in the Environmental Protection Agency report:
   a. _____
   b. _____
   c. _____

3. Impact of *Valdez* oil spill on other parts of the United States:
   a. place where gas prices have increased: _____
   b. how much prices have increased: _____
   c. reason for the price increases: _____

Language Focus

GETTING THE MEANING FROM CONTEXT

22:15-
26:15

Read the excerpts below. View the video again, paying special attention to the *italicized* words or expressions below. Select the best synonym for each.

If you can remember what it was like waiting on those long lines at the gas station ten years ago, if you can see and touch and smell the oil tonight in Valdez Harbor, you might *appreciate* even more the *dilemma* and the debate.

1. *appreciate:*
   a. participate in
   b. pay less attention to
   c. understand
   d. ignore

2. *dilemma:*
   a. ability to choose
   b. easy choice
   c. advantage
   d. difficult choice

The oil from the Exxon Valdez has *fouled* the backyard of Jim and Nancy Lethcoe, *literally*.

3. *fouled:*
   a. made dirty or impure
   b. cleaned
   c. closed
   d. increased the price of

4. *literally:*
   a. largely
   b. actually
   c. strangely
   d. for a long time

Supporters say if we do not drill in ANWR . . . we will again *be hostage to* the Arab oil nations. . . . To them the accident was an *aberration*.

5. *be hostage to:*
   a. act unfriendly
   b. be friendly
   c. be in the power of
   d. entertain

6. *aberration:*
   a. truth
   b. lie
   c. normal situation
   d. unusual event

Rusty oil drums, unprotected from wet or cold, some of them corroded and leaking; *unmonitored* waste disposal, some in an open *pit*.

7. *unmonitored:*
   a. supervised
   b. not checked
   c. dirty
   d. not wanted

8. *pit:*
   a. hole
   b. river
   c. lake
   d. hill

That is likely to be the environmentalists' new *rallying cry* as the evidence *mounts* here at Valdez that the oil companies made promises they did not keep.

9. *rallying cry:*
   a. sad phrase
   b. phrase used to express pain
   c. happy phrase
   d. phrase used to gather support

10. *mounts:*
   a. becomes greater
   b. stays the same
   c. becomes smaller
   d. disappears

That's why many Alaskans, including some oil workers, feel *let down*. Athena Zecevic is married to a pipeline employee and believes oil and nature can mix, but word of the spill has *hit hard*.

11. *let down:*
   a. happy
   b. hopeful
   c. disappointed
   d. confused

12. *hit hard:*
   a. traveled fast
   b. caused pain
   c. traveled slowly
   d. been silenced

There is an oil slick here, a sense of *betrayal* and a *looming* question about the future of drilling in this *remarkable* land.

13. *betrayal:*
   a. disloyalty
   b. wonder
   c. protection
   d. humor

14. *looming:*
    a. strange
    b. foolish
    c. threatening
    d. illegal
15. *remarkable:*
    a. flat
    b. ugly
    c. unusual
    d. common

WORD SCRAMBLE

Unscramble the letters to make a word to fit the definition. All the words are used on the video.

1. mineral oil used to produce gasoline (LORMUTEEP) __ __ __ __ __ __ . __ __ __ __
2. underground tube for carrying gas (PELNIEPI) __ __ __ __ __ __ __ __
3. place giving protection or shelter from danger (GEERUF) __ __ __ __ __ __
4. large ships for carrying oil (KRASTEN) __ __ __ __ __ __ __
5. round containers for oil (USMDR) __ __ __ __ __

Postviewing

WHAT DO YOU THINK?

Write your answers to the following questions. Then discuss your answers with the class.

1. What have you learned from this video?

    _____

    _____

2. Do you think people should be angry at the Exxon oil company for the damage caused by the spill in Prince William Sound? Why or why not?

    _____

    _____

3. Do you think companies should continue to drill for oil in Alaska, even at risk to the environment? Why or why not?

    _____

    _____

4. Do you know of any other major oil spills that have taken place in the world? If so, which ones?

_____

_____

5. Sometimes oil companies violate the laws for potentially hazardous waste. Why do you think this happens?

_____

_____

6. What suggestion can you make to encourage oil companies to obey laws designed to protect the environment?

_____

_____

READING FOR INSIGHT

Read the article below from the *New York Times*, and then answer the questions that follow.

Valdez Spill Toll is Now Called Far Worse

ANCHORAGE, April 17 (AP) — Fish, marine mammals and other resources were harmed much more extensively by the *Exxon Valdez* oil spill than many marine biologists have believed, and the damage is continuing, a new report by state and Federal officials concludes.

The report, a draft of a plan for the long-term restoration of the region affected by the spill, describes extensive damage to sea otters, killer whales, harbor seals, seabirds and fish, a result not only of the spill's immediate effects but also of oil remaining in Prince William Sound.

The plan, issued Thursday, was prepared by the *Exxon Valdez* Oil Spill Trustee Council, made up of six Federal and state officials who are overseeing the spill restoration effort.

The report contradicts a national advertising campaign, conducted over the last year by Exxon, contending that the sound's ecological vitality has been restored to the pristine conditions that prevailed before the tanker *Exxon Valdez* spilled almost 11 million gallons of crude oil there on March 24, 1989.

The report also reflects the concerns of some biologists who have long held that some of the worst damage from the spill would not show up until years after the accident, as the effect of oil worked its way through fish-spawning and animal-breeding cycles.

"I don't want to go to war with Exxon," said Curtis McVee, one of the six trustees who issued the report. "In a general sense, Prince William Sound has recovered, is recovering. But we have specific components of the ecosystem where we still have some concern."

Exxon said Thursday that its officials would not comment on the report until today. But today, the company said that officials who could respond were taking Good Friday off.

Exxon has spent $2.5 billion to clean up the spilled oil. In addition, the company agreed last October to settle court cases resulting from the spill by paying $900 million over 11 years to restore Prince William Sound, $100 million in restitution — half to the state and half to the Federal Government—and a $25 million criminal fine.

Among the findings in the report are these:

• Between 3,500 and 5,000 sea otters died of acute petroleum poisoning. Otter carcasses were found on beaches in 1990 and 1991, and recent surveys indicate a continuing decline in the sound's otter population.

• A significant number of killer whales, or orcas, are missing from at least one and possibly two pods that are known in the sound, and the social structure of the pods appears to be breaking down, with some mothers even abandoning their calves. . . .

• Thousands of bald eagles, sea ducks, loons, cormorants and other species have died, and oil continues to disrupt bird nesting sites....

The report said the spill had affected migrations of salmon fry, major migrations of birds and the primary reproductive period for most species of birds, mammals, fish and marine invertebrate species.

Reprinted with permission from *THE NEW YORK TIMES*, April 18, 1992, p. 6. © 1991 by The New York Times Company.

COMPREHENSION QUESTIONS

1. What did the report prepared by the *Exxon Valdez* Oil Spill Trustee Council conclude?

   _____

   _____

2. What did the advertising campaign conducted by Exxon maintain?

   _____

   _____

3. How did the report reflect the concerns of some biologists?

   _____

   _____

4. What is Curtis McVee's opinion about the recovery of Prince William Sound?

_____

_____

5. What is the total cost of the accident to Exxon—in clean-up, restoration, restitution, and criminal fines?

_____

_____

6. How do you think Exxon officials will respond to the report—if and when they do respond?

_____

_____

RELATED READING: LEARNING ABOUT OIL SPILLS

Read the excerpt from Jon Naar's *Design for a Livable Planet* for two purposes: (1) to learn more about the extent of oil spills in United States waters, and (2) to learn more about the extent of oil spills in other parts of the world. Then fill in the notetaking form that follows.

Oil and Water Don't Mix

When the oil tanker *Exxon Valdez* ran aground in March 1989, dumping 11 million gallons of crude oil into Alaska's Prince William Sound in the largest spill in U.S. history, it was an ecological disaster of epic proportions. In addition to killing untold thousands of birds, fish, and sea otters, the spill threatens the survival of zooplankton, the microorganisms that form the basis of the food chain for all marine creatures.

As it was later revealed, the *Valdez* spill was only one of thousands of oil spills a year—another Exxon tanker had spilled crude oil 15 miles from Waikiki Beach, Hawaii, just three weeks before the Prince William Sound disaster; in January 1989 an Argentine navy supply ship leaked thousands of gallons of diesel oil in Arthur Harbor in the Antarctic; and in late June there were three substantial oil spills within hours of each other. . . . In April of the same year a supertanker ran aground in the Red Sea, leaking nearly a million gallons of oil and imperiling coral reefs and turtle breeding grounds. . . . In January 1990 the Iranian supertanker *Kharg-5* exploded, spilling 20 million gallons of crude oil along the Moroccan coast.

In 1988 alone there were 5,000 to 6,000 spills involving oil and other toxic substances along the coasts and other navigable waters of the U.S. . . . Of these, 12 were classified as major because they involved more than 100,000 gallons. Between 1980 and 1986, 91 million gallons of oil and 36 million gallons of other toxic substances were recorded as being spilled into U.S. waters.

World's Worst Oil Spills

1. February 1983—Nowruz oil field, Persian Gulf, offshore well collapses: estimated spill of 220 million gallons
2. June 1979—Ixtoc 1 oil well explodes in Bay of Campeche near the Yucatán Peninsula, Mexico: 200 million gallons
3. July 1979—Collision of *Atlantic Empress* and *Aegean Captain* off Trinidad: 110 million gallons
4. August 1983—Fire aboard *Castillo de Beliver* off Cape Town, South Africa: 75 million gallons
5. March 1978—*Amoco Cadiz* runs aground off Britanny, France: 70 million gallons
6. March 1967—*Torrey Canyon* runs aground off Land's End, England: 36 million gallons
7. February 1980—*Irene's Serenade* catches fire and sinks off Pylos, Greece: 35 million gallons

Reprinted with permission from *Design for a Livable Planet: How You Can Help Clean Up the Environment*, by Jon Naar, 1990, Harper & Row, p.63.

I. Oil Spills in United States waters

   A. *Exxon Valdez* (largest spill in the United States)

      1. Number of gallons spilled: _____

      2. Forms of life affected: _____

   B. Oil spills in 1988

      1. Total number of spills: _____

      2. Number of major spills: _____

   C. Spills between 1980 and 1986

      1. Number of gallons of oil spilled: _____

      2. Number of gallons of other toxic substances spilled: _____

II. Oil spills in other parts of the world

   A. Largest

      1. Place the spill occurred: _____

      2. Number of gallons spilled: _____

      3. Cause of the spill: _____

   B. Other places around the world affected by major oil spills since 1967:

      1. _____   6. _____

      2. _____   7. _____

      3. _____   8. _____

      4. _____   9. _____

      5. _____

WRITE A LETTER

Write a letter to the Exxon oil company. Describe your reaction to the Prince William Sound disaster and say what you think should be done about it.

FINAL TASK: ROLE PLAY

Work in pairs. One student will play the role of Susan. The other student will play the role of Susan's father. Read the situation and role descriptions below and decide who will play each role. After a ten-minute preparation, begin the discussion between Susan and her father.

The Situation: A Family Discussion

Susan is a student at Ridley College. Last week she heard that the students at Ridley are planning to demonstrate against the oil company where her father works as an executive. The company uses single-bottom oil tankers, and the students are organizing a protest march to demand that the company use double-bottom tankers to reduce the risk of oil spills. Susan plans to participate in the protest march. Tomorrow she will talk to her father about her plans.

ROLE DESCRIPTION: SUSAN

Last summer you spent your vacation visiting a cousin in Santa Barbara, California. While you were there you saw the damage that an oil spill had done to the area. Birds had died because oil had stuck to their wings, making it impossible for them to fly. It seemed like the oil stuck to everything it touched and it was impossible to remove. You were disappointed because you couldn't go sailing or swimming because of the large amount of oil in the water. You now think participating in the protest march is the best way to show your concern.

ROLE DESCRIPTION: SUSAN'S FATHER

You are an executive at a large oil company. You feel that people outside the oil industry have no right to influence oil company policy. You also feel that the use of double-bottom tankers will make home-fuel oil costs extremely high and cause hardship to many people. You think this should affect Susan's attitude.

Segment 6

Ocean Plastic Pollution

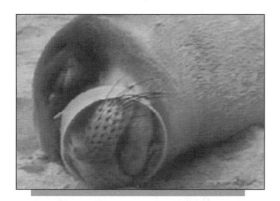

from: *World News Tonight*, 9/6/88
Runtime: 3:57
Begin: 26:51

Previewing

KEY QUESTIONS

1. How widespread is the problem of ocean plastic pollution?
2. How does ocean plastic pollution affect wildlife?
3. What are governments doing to reduce the amount of plastics in the ocean?
4. What can you do to help?

WHAT DO YOU ALREADY KNOW?

What do you already know about plastics in the ocean? Circle the letter of the answer you think is correct. (The answers are on page 62.)

1. What percent of the trash floating in the world's oceans is plastic?
   a. At least 30%.
   b. At least 45%.
   c. At least 60%.
   d. At least 75%.

2. How many fur seals die each year as a result of getting caught in plastic nets and ropes?
   a. About 30,000.
   b. About 40,000.
   c. About 50,000.
   d. About 60,000.

3. How much trash do commercial and merchant fishing vessels dump into the world's oceans each year?
   a. At least 1.3 million pounds.
   b. At least 13 million pounds.
   c. At least 130 million pounds.
   d. At 13 billion pounds.

4. Where does international law prohibit ships from dumping plastics?
   a. Anywhere at sea.
   b. Less than 3 miles offshore.
   c. Less than 12 miles offshore.
   d. Less than 25 miles offshore.

ESSENTIAL WORDS TO KNOW

The *italicized* words in each of the following sentences are all used on the video. Read the sentences and suggest your own definition for each word.

1. The houses along the shore suffered water damage from the *deluge*.
   deluge: _____

2. After the air crash, rescue workers searched the *debris* for survivors.
   debris: _____

3. When the food went down her throat, she started to *choke*.
   choke: _____

4. The animal died because it had *ingested* poison.
   ingest: _____

5. The doctor *autopsied* the body to determine the cause of death.
   autopsy (v): _____

6. It may take hundreds of years for some plastics to *degrade*.
   degrade: _____

PREDICTION

Work in groups. Based on the title of the segment, *Ocean Plastic Pollution*, and your own background knowledge, what do you think you will see and hear on the video? Write down three items under each of the headings on the next page.

Answers: 1. d   2. a   3. d   4. a

SIGHTS (things you expect to see)	WORDS (words you expect to hear)	SOUNDS (sounds you expect to hear)
1. _____	_____	_____
2. _____	_____	_____
3. _____	_____	_____

Global Viewing

CONFIRMING YOUR PREDICTIONS

Go back to the prediction exercise on page 62. Watch the video segment and circle any of your predictions that were mentioned.

27:05-30:00

COMPREHENSION CHECK

Watch the video. As you watch, decide if the statements below are true (*T*) or false (*F*). If the answer is not given on the video, write *NG*.

27:05-30:00

_____ 1. Most of the trash on the beaches in Texas has been dumped there by beachgoers.

_____ 2. People of all nationalities spend their vacations on the Texas Gulf Coast.

_____ 3. Discarded plastics in the oceans are killing seals, turtles, and other wildlife.

_____ 4. The U.S. government is increasing its efforts to solve the problem of plastics in the ocean.

_____ 5. Japan, Russia, and Sweden have signed a new treaty to prohibit dumping plastics in the ocean.

_____ 6. The plastic that is already in the ocean could continue to wash up for the next 100 years.

Intensive Viewing

LISTENING CLOZE

The passage below is from the first part of the video. Watch this part of the video again and fill in the blanks with the missing words.

27:05-28:25

Peter Jennings: Now we have our second report this week in our series on the environment which we call "The _____ of America." As any of us who spent any time on the _____ at all know, it is no longer a _____ to run across something plastic floating in it.

The French oceanographer Jacques Cousteau has found plastic
_____ floating in the Antarctic. One of the
_____ stretches of water anywhere is along the east coast
of Texas. And here's ABC's Al Dale.

Al Dale: The Texas Gulf Coast off Corpus Christi, beautiful vacation land,
ugly eyesore. The _____ here is plastic.

Linda Maranis: You can find anything you want on a Texas beach— from
a _____ to a toilet seat.

Al Dale: It is an unrelenting deluge of debris. Trash made to last, most of it
dumped from _____ , washing up from all over the world.

John Hunter: We have stuff from the _____ . We have stuff from
_____ ships. Almost any nationality can be found on this
shore.

Al Dale: Lightweight plastic, with a life span of hundreds of years,
revolutionized packaging and other _____ in the years
since World War II. This scene from a 1967 movie portrayed it as the
wave of the _____ .

Man: One _____ .

Dustin Hoffman: Yes, sir.

Man: Are you listening?

Dustin Hoffman: Yes, sir. I am.

Man: _____ .

NOTETAKING

28:25-
29:50

Watch the rest of the video and take brief notes on the answers to the
questions below. Then compare your answers with those of another
student. If you disagree, watch the video again.

1. What are researchers at the University of Texas Marine Science Institute
    counting and cataloguing, and why?

    _____

    _____

2. According to Pam Plotkin, who are the polluters?

_____

_____

3. What are some ways that plastic kills wildlife?

_____

_____

4. What percent of the turtles autopsied by Pam Plotkin over the past two years had swallowed plastic?

_____

_____

5. What evidence is there that people are becoming more concerned about the problem of plastics in the ocean?

_____

_____

Language Focus

PHRASAL VERBS

The sentences below are all spoken on the video. Complete each sentence with a phrasal verb from the list. Be sure to change the verb tense if necessary. When you finish, watch the video again and check your answers.

27:10-29:40

call for	keep track	run across	wash up

1. As any of us who has spent any time on the water at all know, it is no longer a surprise to _____ something plastic floating in it.

2. Researchers from the University of Texas Marine Science Institute are trying to _____ of plastic that _____ on Mustang Island.

3. Bills have been introduced in Congress to tighten restrictions on disposals of plastic and _____ expanded use of new plastics that degrade in weeks or months instead of centuries.

VOCABULARY CHECK

The sentences below are from the video segment. Match the *italicized* words and expressions with their equivalents from the list.

a. not slowing down or lessening in amount, speed, intensity, etc.

b. cause (a rule or law) to be carried out

c. scientist that studies the effect of oceans on the earth as a whole

d. plans for laws, written down for a government to consider

e. something very unpleasant to look at

f. follow the course, line, history, development, etc., of

_____ 1. The French *oceanographer* Jacques Cousteau has found plastic bottles floating in the Antarctic.

_____ 2. The Texas Gulf Coast off Corpus Christi—beautiful vacation land, ugly *eyesore*.

_____ 3. It is an *unrelenting* deluge of debris.

_____ 4. Counting and cataloguing it with a computer, they hope, will help *trace* the plastic and lead to solutions.

_____ 5. *Bills* have been introduced in Congress to tighten restrictions.

_____ 6. A treaty goes into effect at the end of this year prohibiting the dumping of plastic at sea, a treaty that will be hard to *enforce*.

WORD PUZZLE 1

Write the answers to the clues in the boxes and circles. All of the words are used on the video.

1. Animals sometimes choke _____ plastic bags.
2. Salt water that covers the greater part of the earth's surface
3. Law being considered by government lawmakers
4. Large state in the southwestern part of the United States
5. Another name for Asia or the Far East
6. Scandinavian nationality
7. Group of elected persons who make the laws of the United States
8. Men who catch fish, as a sport or for a job
9. Large shell-backed reptiles that live in the ocean (two words)

1. ⚪◻
2. ⚪◻◻
3. ⚪◻◻◻
4. ⚪◻◻◻◻
5. ⚪◻◻◻◻◻
6. ◻◻◻◻◻◻⚪
7. ◻◻◻◻⚪◻◻◻
8. ◻◻◻⚪◻◻◻◻◻
9. ◻◻◻◻⚪◻⚪◻◻◻

WORD PUZZLE 2: CIRCLE CLUES

Rearrange the circle clues in the puzzle on page 66 to give you the keyword, which names an everyday plastic item you can find on a Texas beach.

The keyword is __ __ __ __ __ __ __ __ __ .

WORD FORMS

Choose the correct word form to complete each sentence.

1. *restrictions*   *restrict*
   a. New laws could _____ the production of plastic.
   b. New laws could also call for _____ on the disposal of plastic.

2. *polluter*   *polluting*
   a. Fishermen are not the only people who are _____ the water.
   b. Nearly everyone who uses the ocean is a _____ .

3. *prohibitions*   *prohibits*
   a. There are _____ against the improper disposal of plastic.
   b. An international treaty _____ dumping plastics in the ocean.

Postviewing

WHAT DO YOU THINK?

Write your answers to the following questions. Then discuss your answers with the class.

1. Do you think the dumping of plastics in the ocean will increase, continue as is, or slow down in the next ten years? Explain your reasons.

   _____

   _____

2. In the place where you live now, is there anything similar to the problem described on the video? If so, what problems exist?

   _____

   _____

3. Besides those shown on the video, what other animals could be harmed by plastics in the ocean?

_____

_____

4. What efforts, if any, do you think should be made to reduce ocean plastic pollution?

_____

_____

READING FOR INSIGHT

Read the article below. Then answer the comprehension and opinion questions that follow and discuss your answers with another student.

Marine Plastic Pollution and MARPOL

The practice of dumping of garbage into the sea is an ancient one. Since the days when people first started to travel on the oceans, the waters of the world have been used as a "trash can" for unwanted waste from ships and boats. Everything that was no longer useful was thrown overboard—from cargo that had turned bad, to human corpses that were buried at sea. Dumping garbage into the ocean is still the most common disposal system used by ships and boats around the world today.

While the disposal system itself has remained the same, the trash that is dumped overboard has changed drastically. Since World War II, floatable products, most of which are synthetic plastics, have been developed. These "floatables," which neither sink nor decompose at sea, are increasingly visible as trash in the marine environment. It is nearly impossible to cross an ocean or go to a beach anywhere in the world without finding trash in the water or on the shore.

Besides their obviously disastrous effect on the natural beauty of waters and coastlines, floatables can cause serious harm to wildlife and vessels alike. Seabirds and fish can mistake plastic pellets for fish eggs and other food, and suffer from malnutrition or poisoning; sea turtles can mistake plastic bags for jellyfish and starve to death; dolphins and whales can get trapped in plastic fishnets and die; and young seals can get their necks caught in plastic six-pack rings or strapping bands and suffocate. Boat engines and propellers are damaged by a wide range of articles that are "lost" at sea.

Efforts are being made to reduce plastic and other types of ocean pollution throughout the world. Annex V of the MARPOL Treaty (pronounced MAR-POLE and short for Marine Pollution) is a new international law for a cleaner, safer marine environment. The law went into effect on December 31, 1988, and so far 39 countries have agreed to abide by its requirements. This law prohibits the disposal of all plastics in the ocean and requires all vessels to carry their own plastic trash into port for proper disposal. In addition, MARPOL has designated some ocean regions as "special areas" where the dumping of any type of garbage (paper, rags, glass, etc.) is prohibited. These special regions are the Mediterranean, the Baltic Sea, the Black Sea, and the Middle Eastern gulf areas.

COMPREHENSION QUESTIONS

1. How long have ships and boats been dumping their garbage at sea?

   _____

   _____

2. What sorts of "trash" do ships and boats throw overboard?

   _____

   _____

3. How has this trash changed in the years since World War II?

   _____

   _____

4. What material are most "floatables" composed of?

   _____

   _____

5. What are some ways these floatables can harm wildlife?

   _____

   _____

6. How can boats and ships be damaged by floatables?

   _____

   _____

7. What is "MARPOL"?

   _____

   _____

8. In what ocean regions of the world is the dumping of all garbage prohibited?

   _____

   _____

IN YOUR OPINION

1. Have you ever visited any of the ocean regions mentioned as "special areas" in the article? If so, where? Describe it and any ocean pollution you saw there.

   _____

   _____

2. Have the waters and coastlines in your home country been affected by pollution? If so, what sorts of things pollute the marine environment?

_____

_____

RELATED READING: WHAT YOU CAN DO

Read the following excerpt from *50 Simple Things You Can Do to Save the Earth*. Then answer the questions that follow.

SNIP SIX-PACK RINGS
During a beach cleanup along 300 miles of Texas shoreline in 1988, 15,600 plastic six-pack rings were found in 3 hours.

BACKGROUND. Plastic six-pack holders—the rings used for canned beer, soft drinks, oil, etc.—have become an ocean hazard to birds and other marine life. How do they get into the water? They're left on the beach by careless sunlovers and wash into the ocean; or they're dumped into our waterways along with tons of other garbage and gradually make their way into the oceans; or they're dumped into seaside landfills and erosion or wind propels them into the water. Once they're floating in the sea, they're hazards to marine life.

DID YOU KNOW
• Six-pack holders are virtually invisible underwater, so marine animals can't avoid them.
• Gulls and terns—birds that frequent recreational areas and dumps near the ocean—sometimes catch one loop around their necks while fishing. Then they snag another loop on a stationary object. Result: they drown or strangle themselves.
• Pelicans catch fish by plunging into the water. Occasionally, one will dive straight into a six-pack ring. Result: the bird ends up with the ring stuck around its bill; unable to open its mouth, it starves to death.
• Young seals and sea lions get the rings caught around their necks. As they grow, the rings get tighter, and the animals suffocate.
Some states now require six-pack rings to be photodegradable—which means they break down in sunlight after 30 days—but that doesn't deal with the short-term problem.

SIMPLE THINGS TO DO
• Before you toss six-pack holders into the garbage, snip each circle with a scissors.
• When you're on the beach, pick up any six-pack rings you find and take them with you. Snip (or snap) them before you throw them away.

Reprinted with permission from *50 Simple Things You Can Do to Save the Earth*, by the EarthWorks Group, 1989, Earthworks Press, p. 21.

70

COMPREHENSION QUESTIONS

1. What are three ways six-pack rings get into the ocean?

   _____

   _____

2. What are three ways birds and other marine life can be harmed by six-pack rings?

   _____

   _____

3. What are two simple things you can do to prevent animals from being harmed by six-pack rings?

   _____

   _____

RELATED READING: HOW YOU CAN HELP

How can you help to solve the marine pollution problem? Read the list of suggestions below. Then discuss the following questions with the class:

1. Which suggestions seem most practical to you?
2. Which suggestions, if any, do you intend to follow?

MARINE POLLUTION: What Can You Do to Help?

Take part in a coastal cleanup campaign.
Avoid buying and using disposal plastic products and packaging.
Keep trash with you when on a boat or a beach, then dispose of it properly.
Educate yourself on marine conservation issues.

Always throw unwanted fishing line in a trash can, not in the water.
Cut loops from six-pack rings before discarding them.
Talk to your family and friends about marine conservation issues.
Implement a curbside recycling program in your community.
Offer your assistance to marine conservation groups.
Notify the Coast Guard if you see recreational or commercial vessels dumping plastics into waterways.

SPECIAL RESEARCH ASSIGNMENT

If you live in a coastal area, visit a beach and make a list of the ten most common types of debris you see in the water or on the beach. How might the various types of debris you found be harmful to wildlife? Write a one-page report summarizing your findings and your recommendations for dealing with the types of debris you found.

WRITE A REACTION

Write a one-page reaction to the statement below.

The permanent solution to pollution lies with each individual; how we as individuals act determines the condition of our environment.

CONDUCT A POLL

Poll eight to ten people to find out their answers to the following question:

Are you concerned about the problem of ocean pollution? Why or why not?

Keep a record of people's responses and note down any interesting comments they make. Tally the responses and summarize your findings in a one-page report. Be sure to include any interesting comments made by the people you interviewed.

FINAL TASK: BRAINSTORMING

Work in groups of three or four. Imagine you are delegates to the International Convention for the Prevention of Ocean Plastic Pollution. Brainstorm your answers to this question:

What steps should government and industry take to eliminate ocean plastic pollution?

Follow this procedure:
1. Choose someone on the team to write down and report the group's ideas.
2. Come up with as many ideas as you can.
3. Report your ideas to the class.
4. Once each group has presented its ideas, select the three best from the entire class.

Segment 7
Earth Summit Snag

from: *American Agenda*, 6/3/92
Runtime: 5:41
Begin: 30:12

Previewing

KEY QUESTIONS
1. What countries are responsible for most of the environmental damage that has already been done to the earth?
2. What countries are likely to be the main polluters in the 21st century?
3. How can developing countries modernize without contributing to environmental pollution?
4. What role, if any, should developed countries play in the developing countries' plans for industrialization?

PREDICTION
Work in groups. The video segment focuses on India and how that country and other large, rapidly developing countries can industrialize and improve the life styles of their people without causing more harm to the environment. Based on your own background knowledge, what do you

think you will see and hear on the video? Write down four items under each of the headings below.

	SIGHTS (things you expect to see)	**WORDS** (words you expect to hear)	**SOUNDS** (sounds you expect to hear)
1.	_____	_____	_____
2.	_____	_____	_____
3.	_____	_____	_____
4.	_____	_____	_____

ESSENTIAL WORDS TO KNOW

The *italicized* words and expressions below are used in the video segment. Familiarize yourself with their meanings, and then write a sentence with the italicized word or expression included.

1. *summit meeting* = an important meeting between two or more heads of state

   _____

2. *environmental degradation* = the reduced quality of the earth's environment as a result of pollution, deforestation, etc.

   _____

3. *refineries* = buildings or places for purifying metals, oil or sugar

   _____

4. *greenhouse gases* = carbon dioxide and other gases which prevent heat from escaping into space

   _____

5. *emissions* = liquids, gases, etc., which are released into the atmosphere

   _____

6. *leverage* = power, influence or some other means of obtaining a desired result

   _____

Global Viewing

30:25-
35:40

CONFIRMING YOUR PREDICTIONS

Go back to the prediction exercise at the top of this page. Watch the video segment and circle any of your predictions that were mentioned.

GETTING THE MAIN IDEAS

Read the following sentences. Then watch the video and check (✓) the sentences that are *true*. Compare your answers with those of another student. If you disagree, watch the video again.

30:25-
35:40

_____ 1. Leaders in India believe that most environmental degradation has been caused by the rich, developed countries.

_____ 2. Cars, refineries and electric plants in India and other poor countries are responsible for most of the carbon dioxide that now threatens the world's climate.

_____ 3. Many people in India would like to have the same kinds of technology that people in developed countries have.

_____ 4. Developing countries want the rich, developed countries to provide them with non-polluting technologies.

_____ 5. It will cost developed countries billions of dollars to provide poor, developing countries with non-polluting technologies.

Intensive Viewing

GETTING THE DETAILS

Read the following questions. Then watch the first part of the video again and choose the correct answer to each question.

30:25-
32:45

1. In what Latin American city was the United Nations Conference on the Environment and Development held?
   a. Mexico City.
   b. Rio de Janeiro.
   c. Caracas.
   d. Buenos Aires.

2. By what other name is the United Nations Conference on the Environment and Development known?
   a. The Earth Summit.
   b. The Conference for a Livable Planet.
   c. The Green Summit.
   d. The Summit to Save the Planet.

3. How many nations were represented at the conference?
   a. 7
   b. 70
   c. 117
   d. 170

4. What is the name of the man who organized the conference?
   a. Kamal Nath.
   b. Ned Potter.
   c. Maurice Strong.
   d. Jacques-Yves Cousteau.

5. What is the population of India?
   a. 850,000
   b. 8,500,000
   c. 85,000,000
   d. 850,000,000

6. What is the name of the Indian minister of the environment?
   a. Anil Agawal.
   b. Maurice Strong.
   c. Mahatma Gandhi.
   d. Kamal Nath.

7. According to Ned Potter, what will happen to India within the next 30 years?
   a. Its population will decrease.
   b. It will become a major polluter.
   c. It will eliminate pollution.
   d. It will reduce its global warming emissions.

8. What country is expected to mine half the world's coal within the next 30 years?
   a. India.
   b. The United States.
   c. Russia.
   d. China.

NOTETAKING

33:00-
35:05

Watch the next part of the video again and take brief notes on the answers to the questions below. Then compare your answers with those of another student. If you disagree, watch the video again.

1. Why is it difficult for India to develop without becoming a major producer of greenhouse gases?

   _____

   _____

2. What are some consumer goods that India's citizens are demanding?

_____

_____

3. What sort of treaty did the Western nations at the Earth Summit want the Asian countries to sign?

_____

_____

4. Why did the Asians refuse to sign the treaty?

_____

_____

5. How much money do the developing countries owe to the developed countries?

_____

_____

6. What do the developing countries have as leverage in their argument to persuade the Western countries to provide them with non-polluting technologies?

_____

_____

LISTENING CLOZE

The passage below is from the last part of the video transcript. View the last part of the video again and fill in the blanks with the missing words.

35:05-35:20

Ashok Khosla: If the poor continue to destroy their _____ because they have to _____ , to destroy their _____ and their _____ because they have to _____ , sooner or later that is going to show up in global processes like climate _____ .

Ned Potter: _____ countries say the way out is for _____ countries to provide them with non-polluting technologies. But that will take _____ of dollars, sure to be argued _____ at the summit. For now, the _____ and developing _____ may be far apart, but each controls the other's _____ . Ned Potter, ABC News, New Delhi.

Language Focus

VOCABULARY CHECK

The sentences below are from the video segment. Match the *italicized* words and expressions with their equivalents from the list.

a. the state or condition of being very poor

b. absolute

c. drinking or using up large amounts quickly

d. easy winner in a race, competition, etc.

e. advantages

f. give up or do without

_____ 1. Many of the so-called developing nations of the world believe they are being asked to give up the *benefits* of a modern industrial nation.

_____ 2. The so-called Third World could become a *runaway first* in producing greenhouse gases.

_____ 3. It will be especially difficult because as India's economy grows, millions of its people are demanding energy *guzzling* consumer goods.

_____ 4. Many Indians argue that they cannot be made to *forgo* industrialization just because the West says so.

_____ 5. It would be a crisis because developing nations see timber exports as a way out of *poverty*.

_____ 6. By *sheer* size, they can shape the future of the world's environment.

30:40-
34:35

GETTING THE MEANING FROM CONTEXT

Read the excerpts below. Then view the video again, paying special attention to the *italicized* words and expressions. Choose the best definition for each.

They have a very *tall order*—how to prevent making the place we live in an unlivable place.

1. *tall order*:
    a. long list
    b. easy job
    c. difficult task
    d. loud command

2. *unlivable*:
    a. easy to live in
    b. hard to live in
    c. dead
    d. impossible to live in

The countries there have very different ideas about how to save the planet, and there's a very *fundamental dispute* which is unlikely to be resolved.

3. *fundamental dispute*:
   a. basic argument
   b. violent argument
   c. unimportant argument
   d. silly argument

This is a *prime* issue for the Earth Summit—how poor countries like India can develop without *overwhelming* us all.

4. *prime*:
   a. major
   b. minor
   c. normal
   d. unusual

5. *overwhelming*:
   a. improving
   b. destroying
   c. asking
   d. responding to

It would be a crisis because developing nations see timber exports as a way out of poverty to pay the trillion-dollar *debt* they owe to the wealthy industrial countries.

6. *debt*:
   a. prize
   b. gift
   c. treaty
   d. something one has to pay

PHRASAL VERBS

The sentences below are all spoken on the video. Choose the correct phrasal verb to complete each sentence. Be sure to change the verb tense if necessary. When you finish, watch the video and check your answers.

31:10-
35:19

| cut down | cut off | give up | show up | turn to |

1. Many of the so-called developing nations of the world believe that they are being asked to _____ the benefits of a modern industrial nation.

2. So many of India's people want the same kinds of technology we have, and as all those bicycles _____ cars, that will mean more and more greenhouse gases.

3. For instance, look at rain forests, which India and other countries are _____ , but which the Western countries want saved because they absorb global warming gases.

4. Now they say those same countries, which they often call "The North," are trying to make them sign environmental treaties that _____ their hope of wealth.

5. If the poor continue to destroy their forests because they have to live, to destroy their waters and their soils because they have to survive, sooner or later that is going to _____ in global processes like climate change.

WORD FORMS

The sentences below are from the video segment. The words in italics are either nouns, verbs or adjectives. Complete the grid below by adding the other forms of the *italicized* word.

1. The summit opened with a warning from the man who *organized* it.
2. Many of the so-called developing nations of the world believe that they are being asked to give up the benefits of a modern *industrial* nation.
3. The U.S., Europe and the other rich countries with their cars, refineries and electric plants *emit* most of the carbon dioxide that threatens the climate, but the balance is quickly changing.
4. For instance, look at rain forests, which India and other countries are cutting down, but which the Western countries want saved because they *absorb* global warming gases.
5. If the poor countries continue to destroy their forests because they have to live, to destroy their waters and their soils because they have to *survive*, sooner or later that is going to show up in global processes like climate change.

	NOUN	VERB	ADJECTIVE
1.	_____	organized	_____
2.	_____	_____	industrial
3.	_____	emit	_____
4.	_____	absorb	_____
5.	_____	survive	_____

Postviewing

WHAT DO YOU THINK?

Write your answers to the following questions. Then discuss your answers with the class.

1. What have you learned from this video?

   _____

   _____

2. What is your reaction to people in India demanding energy-consuming goods such as air conditioners, color TVs and washing machines?

   _____

   _____

3. Do you think that the creation of pollution is an inevitable result of industrialization, or can it be prevented? Explain your answer.

   _____

   _____

4. What is your reaction to the rich industrialized nations trying to get poor Asian countries to sign environmental treaties that cut off these poorer countries' hopes of wealth?

   _____

   _____

5. Do you think rich countries should provide poor countries with non-polluting technologies? Why or why not?

   _____

   _____

6. Has anything been done in your home country to reduce the pollution caused by cars, refineries or electric plants? If so, what?

   _____

   _____

RELATED READING: A CASE STUDY

The video focuses on India. The article on the next page focuses on development and related problems in another giant country—China. Read the article. Then answer the comprehension and opinion questions that follow and discuss your answers with other students.

Case Study: China

At 1.1 billion, China's population ranks first in the world and represents 21% of the human species. Until 1980, it was also among the world's most rapidly growing populations. However, effective programs in family planning, health and education have allowed China to cut its rate of population growth in half.

In the 1970s, when the population neared one billion, China's leaders came to the conclusion that rapid population growth was preventing economic development. The country faced enormous problems in trying to provide all those people with food, clothing, housing, education and employment in a crowded and resource-depleted land. In 1979, in an effort to deal with these development-related problems, the Chinese government introduced its famous one-child policy. Parents who agree to have only one child are offered incentives in the form of higher salaries, better housing and better educational opportunities for their only child. Families with more than one child are fined up to $2,000 and can be fired from their jobs.

The program has been largely successful by world standards, especially in the cities. In 1987, 96% of the couples in Shanghai who were expecting their first child agreed to make that baby their last. However, the one-child policy has met with some opposition in the countryside. This is partly due to the fact that rural families, many of whom are farmers, depend on children to help out on the land and to ensure a better chance of survival. Another factor is the traditional preference for boys, who can take over family responsibilities when the parents die.

While China has managed to reduce its rate of population growth, it still has not solved all its problems. Widespread and inefficient use of coal as an energy source (in addition to locally cut fuelwood) has resulted in severe environmental problems such as air pollution and acid rain. The country has enormous coal reserves, and if its energy use ever reaches a level comparable to that of the developed nations, the results will be catastrophic—for China and the rest of the world. One of the world's most serious problems is to find ways for countries like China to develop without making the earth unlivable.

COMPREHENSION QUESTIONS

1. What kinds of problems caused China's leaders to introduce the one-child policy?

   _____

   _____

2. Where has the one-child policy been most successful?

   _____

   _____

3. Where, and for what reasons, has the one-child policy met with some opposition?

_____

_____

4. What is responsible for China's air pollution and acid rain problems?

_____

_____

IN YOUR OPINION

1. Do you think China's one-child policy is a good idea? Why or why not?

_____

_____

2. In your opinion, do governments have a right to limit the number of children a couple will have? Why or why not?

_____

_____

3. Would a one-child policy be acceptable in your home country? Why or why not?

_____

_____

4. If the government in the country in which you are now living introduced a one-child policy, would you agree to it? Why or why not?

_____

_____

WRITE A REACTION

Write a one-page reaction to the following statement. You may agree or disagree with it.

Global warming, pollution, deforestation and other environmental problems are rooted in over-population. Most environmental problems would be solved if we limited world population growth.

MINI-RESEARCH TASK

Listed below are five countries with environmental problems. Using magazines, books and newspapers, find out the following information about each country: (1) location; (2) population; (3) major industries and natural resources; (4) major energy sources; and (5) pollution or other environmental problems. Write a paragraph or two about each country. Also, write a summary sentence or two that describe what they all have in common.

1. Bangladesh
2. Congo
3. Czechoslovakia
4. Ethiopia
5. Mexico

FINAL TASK: BRAINSTORMING

Work in groups of three or four. Imagine you are delegates to the Earth Summit in Rio de Janeiro. Brainstorm your answers to the following question:

What can be done to help the larger, poor developing countries like India and China develop without causing further damage to the environment?

Follow this procedure:

1. Choose someone on the team to write down and report the group's ideas.
2. Come up with as many ideas as you can.
3. Report your ideas to the class.
4. Once each group has presented its ideas, select the three best from the entire class.

Segment 8

Scientists Seek Proof Positive of Global Warming Effects

from: *American Agenda*, 6/9/92
Runtime: 5:45
Begin: 35:55

Previewing

KEY QUESTIONS

1. Where do scientists look for evidence of global warming?
2. What kind of evidence have they found?
3. Why do scientists disagree about the potential effects of global warming?
4. What do environmentalists think should be done about global warming?

WHAT DO YOU ALREADY KNOW?

The topic of the video segment is global warming. Write down your answers to the following questions. Then compare your answers with those of another student.

1. What do you already know about global warming?

   _____

   _____

2. What are you unsure of about global warming?

   _____

   _____

3. What do you hope to learn about global warming?

   _____

   _____

ESSENTIAL WORDS TO KNOW

The *italicized* words in the sentences below are used on the video. Read the sentences and then match the words with their meanings.

algae: Marine biologists use a microscope to examine *algae*.
bleaching: We put the towels in the washing machine for another *bleaching*.
shift (v):   The wind *shifted* its direction from the south to the west.
orchid: I gave my mother a bouquet of *orchids* for her birthday.
ecosystem: Deserts, forests and grasslands are very large *ecosystems*.
dissipate: As soon as the sun came out, the mist *dissipated*.

_____ 1. algae   a. a habitat and all the species that inhabit it
_____ 2. bleaching b. to move or change
_____ 3. shift   c. very simple, small plants living in or near water
_____ 4. orchid   d. a kind of plant with very showy flowers
_____ 5. ecosystem e. to disappear or spread out in different directions
_____ 6. dissipate f. whitening or lightening in color

PREDICTION

In Peter Jenning's introduction to the news story he asks, "How do we know there really is a danger of global warming?" Based on his question and your own background knowledge, predict the kinds of information you think will be included on the video segment.

1. _____

2. _____

3. _____

4. _____

5. _____

Global Viewing

SOUND OFF

36:43-
37:25

Watch the first minute of the news story with the sound turned off. Then answer the following questions. When you finish answering the questions, compare your answers with those of another student.

1. What is the occupation of the divers?

_____

_____

2. What are they looking for underwater?

_____

_____

3. What do you think the woman is talking about?

_____

_____

CHECKING YOUR ANSWERS

Now watch the first minute of the news story with the sound turned on. Which of your answers in the Sound Off exercise were correct?

36:43-
37:25

GETTING THE GENERAL IDEA

Watch the entire video segment. Then write brief answers to the questions below. When you finish, compare your answers with those of another student.

36:09-
40:45

1. What are some places scientists look for early signals of global warming?

_____

_____

2. What are some instruments they use to collect and analyze their data?

_____

_____

3. What are some examples of evidence they have already found?

_____

_____

4. What are some things that might prevent global warming from actually happening?

_____

_____

Intensive Viewing

TRUE OR FALSE?

Read the sentences below. Then watch the first part of the news story. As you watch, decide whether each statement is true or false. Write _T_ or _F_.

36:45-
37:25

_____ 1. The coral reef around the Florida Keys is normally darkened by algae.

_____ 2. The water around the Florida Keys has been colder than normal for more than a decade.

_____ 3. Warm water forces the algae out of the water and leaves some patches of coral bleached.

_____ 4. In Tundi Agardy's opinion, coral bleaching is a sign of greenhouse warming.

_____ 5. According to Tundi Agardy, scientists have seen coral bleaching everywhere in the world.

LISTENING FOR DETAILS

37:26-
38:35

Watch the next part of the video and choose the best answer for each of the following questions.

1. According to Ned Potter, there is fairly little scientific debate about _____
   a. whether global warming is an issue.
   b. how soon we are most likely to feel global warming.
   c. how severe the effects of global warming will be.
   d. in what ways global warming will affect us.

2. What are "greenhouse signals"?
   a. Actions to prevent global warming.
   b. Scientific experiments conducted in a greenhouse.
   c. Ecological changes related to global warming.
   d. Road signs pointing the way to a greenhouse.

3. Dr. Xiao-Hai Yan says the warm spot in the Pacific Ocean has grown warmer and larger because of _____
   a. algae and regional weather patterns.
   b. algae and greenhouse warming.
   c. regional weather patterns and satellites.
   d. regional weather patterns and greenhouse warming.

4. What have scientists at the University of Michigan been documenting?
   a. Plant species whose habitats have been shifting.
   b. Animal species whose habitats have been shifting.
   c. Both a and b.
   d. Plant and animal species that have become extinct.

5. Which of the following is NOT true about the orchid shown on the video?
   a. Its habitat has shifted.
   b. It dies in hot weather.
   c. It can now be found in the region shown on the map.
   d. It has moved northward.

6. James Teeri says species that are shifting northward _____ early indicators that ecosystems are beginning to respond to climate change.
   a. are definitely
   b. may be
   c. never have been
   d. could not possibly be

LISTENING CLOZE
Watch this part of the video and fill in the blanks with the missing words.

38:35-40:00

Ned Potter: The key phrase there is "may be," because for every sign that suggests greenhouse warming there is another to cloud the picture. Clouds themselves are a question mark. In a greenhouse world, more _____ would form. But would they shield us from the sun's _____ or trap more of it close to the _____ ? Likewise, nobody can say how much additional heat the _____ would absorb, or how much we can count on _____ to absorb greenhouse gases. Even smoke from volcanoes, power plants, and the _____ of rain forests may act as a temporary sunshade. That leaves a lot of room for some people to say . . .

S. Fred Singer: Although we should be concerned with the issue, greenhouse warming is essentially a nonproblem for all _____ purposes.

Ned Potter: S. Fred Singer is a scientist who often defends industries like coal and oil, which are less concerned about the _____ than about drastic _____ measures being proposed to protect it.

S. Fred Singer: Any time you try to limit the use of _____ , you're really limiting economic growth.

Ned Potter: At Rio, the U.S. has been mindful of that argument, trying to _____ any agreement it says would cost American jobs. Environmentalists say that's shortsighted, because a few prudent steps like energy efficiency can pay for themselves, even if global warming _____ happens.

Language Focus

EXPRESSING POSSIBILITY

The verbs *may*, *could*, or *might* are often used to express possibility. Rewrite the sentences below using may, could, or might. Use each word twice.

Example: It is possible that there is a danger of global warming.

There $\begin{bmatrix} \text{may} \\ \text{could} \\ \text{might} \end{bmatrix}$ be a danger of global warming.

1. There is a possibility that coral bleaching is a signal of greenhouse warming.

   _____

   _____

2. It's also possible that ocean warming is a greenhouse signal.

   _____

   _____

3. Maybe clouds would shield us from the sun's heat.

   _____

   _____

4. There is a possibility that clouds would actually trap the sun's heat close to the earth.

   _____

   _____

5. Maybe trees would absorb greenhouse gases.

   _____

   _____

6. It's possible that smoke from volcanoes, power plants, and the burning of rain forests would act as a temporary sunshade.

   _____

   _____

36:15-
40:00

GETTING THE MEANING FROM CONTEXT

Read the excerpts below. Then view the video again, paying special attention to the *italicized* words and expressions. Choose the best synonym for each.

As we reported from Rio this evening, with or without the U.S., Europe is going to put very *strict* limits on those gases that have the *potential* at least to *trap* heat in the earth's atmosphere, like a greenhouse. The Bush administration is refusing to do so, because it says the case for global warming is not *compelling* enough to demand that American industries use less oil and gas.

1. *strict*:
   a. weak
   b. severe
   c. cheap
   d. expensive

2. *potential*:
   a. poison
   b. task
   c. possibility
   d. impossibility

3. *trap*:
   a. destroy
   b. reduce
   c. release
   d. catch

4. *compelling*:
   a. strong
   b. weak
   c. profitable
   d. improving

Why look underwater? Because this coral reef *skirting* the Florida *Keys* is normally darkened by algae, but the water here has been warmer than normal over a decade, forcing algae out and leaving some *patches* bleached.

5. *skirting*:
   a. wearing a skirt
   b. covering
   c. lying around the edge of
   d. living in

6. *Keys*:
   a. low islands
   b. high mountains
   c. dried-up rivers
   d. deep valleys

7. *patches*:
   a. areas
   b. small fish
   c. chemicals
   d. holes

So scientists are looking for what they call "greenhouse signals," the first ecological changes that clearly can be *linked* to the warming.

8. *linked*:
   a. harmful
   b. beneficial
   c. separated
   d. connected

One type of orchid . . . could be found in this region 40 years ago, but has now *retreated* north almost a hundred miles.

9. *retreated*:
   a. moved back
   b. advanced
   c. become extinct
   d. been phased out

S. Fred Singer is a scientist who often defends industries like coal and oil which are less concerned about the climate than about *drastic* economic *measures* being proposed to protect it.

10. *drastic:*
   a. moderate
   b. wonderful
   c. very severe
   d. old-fashioned

11. *measures*:
   a. obstacles
   b. products or elements
   c. actions or plans
   d. statements

At Rio, the U.S. has been *mindful* of that argument, trying to stop any agreement it says would *cost* American jobs. Environmentalists say that's *shortsighted*, because a few *prudent* steps like energy efficiency can pay for themselves, even if global warming never happens.

12. *mindful*:
   a. careless
   b. attentive
   c. distrustful
   d. forgetful

13. *cost*:
   a. result in a loss of
   b. result in an increase of
   c. raise the salaries of
   d. reduce the salaries of

14. *shortsighted*:
   a. considering what is likely to happen in the future
   b. not considering what is likely to happen in the future
   c. insufficient
   d. sufficient

15. *prudent*:
   a. careful or wise
   b. impractical
   c. careless
   d. unnecessary

Postviewing

READING FOR INSIGHT

Read the article below to learn more about the causes and potential effects of global warming. Then answer the comprehension and opinion questions that follow and discuss your answers with other students.

GLOBAL FORECAST: HOT—AND GETTING HOTTER

The year 1990 was the hottest ever recorded. Climatologists estimate that the earth's surface temperature has increased by between .5 and $1.25\,^\circ$ F. (-17.5 and $-17.08\,^\circ$ C.) in the past 150 years because of the global warming. Increases of .5 or $1.25\,^\circ$ F. may seem small, but the experts are talking about more than a change in the weather—the daily change in temperature, winds, and precipitation. They are talking about a change in the climate—the average weather over a large area for many years. And it may get hotter. In 1990 a United Nations commission of more than 300 scientists said that if global warming continues unchecked, the earth's average temperature could rise between 6 and $9\,^\circ$ F. (-14.4 and $-12.7\,^\circ$ C.) by the end of the 21st century. What are some of the potential effects of global warming?

• The weather could become hotter and drier. Important farming regions would dry out and become less productive.

• The polar ice caps could melt. As the temperature goes up, the melting of the polar ice caps would cause the sea level to rise several hundred feet. Low-lying land areas such as Cairo and the rice floodplains in southern Asia, and entire countries such as the Netherlands and Bangladesh, would be flooded. Saltwater would flow into freshwater, destroying drinking water and irrigation sources.

• Climate zones could move. A change in temperature of just a few degrees would cause areas favorable for certain plants and animals to move hundreds of miles. Species unable to keep up with the changes might become extinct.

Global warming, sometimes called the "greenhouse effect," is caused by atmospheric gases—such as carbon dioxide, chloroflourocarbons (CFCs) and methane—that trap the sun's heat next to the earth, the way that glass traps heat in a greenhouse. Some of these greenhouse gases are a natural part of the atmosphere. The problem, according to some scientists, is that the greenhouse effect is increasing because of human activities: the cutting down and burning of rain forests, the operating of power plants fueled by coal and oil, and the running of automobile engines fueled by gas (petroleum).

COMPREHENSION QUESTIONS

1. What are some things that could happen if the earth's average temperature rose between 6 and 9 ° F. (–14.4 and –12.7° C.)?

_____

_____

2. How does the greenhouse effect work?

_____

_____

3. What human activities could increase the greenhouse effect?

_____

_____

IN YOUR OPINION

1. If you were a climatologist, what would you like to discover about global warming?

_____

_____

2. To your knowledge, has there been any change in weather patterns in your home country in recent years? If so, describe the change.

_____

_____

CONDUCT A POLL

Poll eight to ten people to learn their opinions on the following question:

Do you think global warming is a serious problem? Why or why not?

Write a one-page summary of their responses. In addition, be prepared to tell the class what you learned from the people you polled.

MINI-RESEARCH TASK

Listed below are some substitutes for energy produced by fossil fuels (coal, oil, and natural gas). Using magazines, books and newspapers, find out some uses for each substitute (running cars, producing electricity, etc.), as well as the advantages and disadvantages of each substitute. Write a one-page summary of the information you obtain.

1. biomass
2. geothermal power
3. hydropower
4. nuclear power
5. solar power
6. windpower

FINAL TASK: DEBATE

Divide the class into two teams: Team A and Team B. Conduct a debate on the issue of global warming. In your team, do the following:

1. Read the background description for your side. Do NOT read the background description for the other team.
2. Prepare your arguments for the debate.
3. Before the debate begins, select a moderator to lead the discussion. Follow the procedure below when conducting the debate.
   A. Team A begins with a three minute presentation.
   B. Team B then gives a three-minute presentation.
   C. Team A gives a three-minute response to Team B's presentation.
   D. Team B gives a three-minute response to Team A's presentation.
   E. The moderator evaluates the strengths of both arguments.

TEAM A

You will take the view of the environmentalists, that governments should act now to prevent global warming. Even though scientists are not absolutely sure of global warming, you believe that governments should take immediate steps to reduce greenhouse gases from getting into the atmosphere. You think if we wait too long, it may be too late to prevent damage from the warming trend. In your opinion, it is better to pay the price now—not later, when the effects of global warming can't be reversed.

TEAM B

You will take the view that governments should wait for more evidence before taking energy reduction measures to prevent global warming. You believe that limiting the use of energy will limit economic growth. In your opinion, governments should wait until scientists are absolutely sure of global warming before taking any actions that might drive some smaller companies out of business or cost people their jobs. You think it's important to keep in mind that many of the predictions about the effects of global warming are based on theory.

Segment 9

Recycling and Other Solutions to the Trash Problem

from: *American Agenda*, 12/2/88
Runtime: 4:47
Begin: 41:01

Previewing

KEY QUESTIONS

1. How much trash do Americans throw away each day?
2. What item do you think they throw out most?
2. Where does the trash go?
3. Who or what is is to blame for the increase in the amount of trash produced?
4. What are some possible solutions to the trash problem?

DISCUSSION

1. What kinds of trash do you throw away every day?

_____

_____

2. Where does your community dump its trash?

_____

_____

3. Who is responsible for collecting the trash in your community—the department of sanitation or a private company?

_____

_____

4. What are some things people can do to reduce the amount of trash they throw away?

_____

_____

PREDICTION

Work in groups. Based on the title of the segment *Recycling and Other Solutions to the Trash Problem* and your own background knowledge, what do you think you will see and hear on the video? Write down four items under each of the headings below.

SIGHTS (things you expect to see)	WORDS (words you expect to hear)	SOUNDS (sounds you expect to hear)
1. _____	_____	_____
2. _____	_____	_____
3. _____	_____	_____
4. _____	_____	_____

ESSENTIAL WORDS TO KNOW

The following words will help you understand the video segment. Try to guess their meanings. Use a dictionary, if necessary. In each group of words, cross out the word that does **not** have a similar meaning to the *italicized* word. Then compare your answers with those of another student. The first one has been done for you.

1. *discard*	~~keep~~	throw away	toss out
2. *debris*	garbage	waste	nature
3. *firm*	company	customer	corporation
4. *tinted*	clear	colored	shaded
5. *tin*	metal	mineral	wood
6. *scrap*	junk	new	used

Global Viewing

CONFIRMING YOUR PREDICTIONS

Go back to the prediction exercise above. Watch the entire segment and circle any of your predictions that were mentioned.

41:15-
45:40

98

GETTING THE MAIN IDEAS

Read the questions below. Then watch the video again and choose the best answer to each question.

42:15-45:20

1. How much trash do Americans throw away?
   a. A billion pounds a minute.
   b. A billion pounds a day.
   c. A billion pounds a week.
   d. A billion pounds a year.

2. What item do Americans throw out most?
   a. Paper.
   b. Plastic.
   c. Metal.
   d. Glass.

3. Who does industry blame for the large amounts of trash produced?
   a Company managers.
   b. Engineers.
   c. Consumers.
   d. The government.

4. What happens to most of the trash generated by Americans?
   a. It is dumped into the sea.
   b. It is burned.
   c. It is recycled by private firms.
   d. It is dumped into a landfill.

5. According to the video, what is the best solution to the trash problem?
   a. Looking for more landfills.
   b. Burning garbage.
   c. Changing packaging.
   d. Recycling.

6. How much of the garbage produced in the United States is recycled?
   a. Ten percent.
   b. Twenty-five percent.
   c. Forty percent.
   d. Fifty percent.

7. How much of the waste produced in the United States CANNOT be reused?
   a. Ten percent.
   b. Twenty-five percent.
   c. Forty percent.
   d. Fifty percent.

Intensive Viewing

LISTENING CLOZE

41:15-
42:05

The passage below is from the first part of the video. Watch the first part of the video again and fill in the blanks with the missing words.

Peter Jennings: And so we come to the end of our third week of American Agenda. When we began we said this segment would focus on issues in our national life which are more _____ than others and therefore worth more _____ . We also said these issues were important because there were _____ which need to be made. Tonight is no exception, but unlike many other issues we've explored already, this _____ is so commonplace that most people just don't see it. Of course, we will not be able to miss the _____ . Here's Ned Potter.

Ned Potter: This is where the story ends—on top of a _____ in Camden County, New Jersey. Sneakers, _____ books, diapers, _____ bags, soda _____ —piled up and shoveled under.

Fred Krupp: We have a throw-away society where many _____ have a useful life of only a few _____ .

TRUE OR FALSE?

42:10-
43:00

Read the sentences below. Then watch the next part of the video. As you watch, decide whether each statement is true or false. Write *T* or *F*.

_____ 1. Americans discard 2.5 million plastic containers an hour.
_____ 2. Other countries throw away more trash than the U.S. does.
_____ 3. Plastic bottles can survive in landfills for hundreds of years.
_____ 4. A third of the Burgoyne family's trash is packaging.
_____ 5. Americans generate more trash now than they did in 1960.

NOTETAKING

Watch the rest of the video and take brief notes on the answers to the questions below. Then compare your answers with those of another student.

43:00-45:05

1. What are some reasons consumers prefer plastic containers?

   _____

   _____

2. Why do companies like Pepsi Cola prefer plastic containers?

   _____

   _____

3. In addition to recycling, Ned Potter mentions the four ideas below as possible solutions to the trash problem. What problem does each of the following solutions present?

   a. Looking for new landfill: _____

   b. Burning garbage: _____

   c. Making plastics biodegradable: _____

   d. Reducing the amount of garbage: _____

4. Why is recycling the best solution to the trash problem?

   _____

   _____

5. Name some materials that can be recycled?

   _____

   _____

Language Focus

RELATIVE CLAUSES

Relative clauses can make the language we use sound more sophisticated. Instead of expressing an idea in two simple sentences that repeat the same noun, we can express the same idea in one sentence by replacing the noun with a relative pronoun like *which* or *that*. This changes two simple sentences into one more complex sentence, as in the following example from the video.

SIMPLE SENTENCES	The recycling company charges the town nothing because it sells the end product to firms. The firms will use it again.
COMPLEX SENTENCE	The recycling company charges the town nothing because it sells the end product to firms (that) will use it again.

101

The following sentences are from the video. Underline the relative clause in each sentence. Then circle the relative pronoun and draw an arrow from it to the noun it describes, as in the example on page 101.

1. When we began we said this segment would focus on issues in our national life which are more important than others and therefore worth more attention.

2. We also said these issues were important because there were choices which need to be made.

3. They buy food in plastic bottles that survive in landfills for centuries.

WORD FORMS

The sentences below are from the video segment. The italicized words are either nouns, verbs, or adjectives. Complete the grid below by adding the other forms of the *italicized* word. When you finish, compare your chart with that of another student.

1. Tonight is no *exception*, but unlike many other issues we've explored already, this problem is so commonplace that most people don't see it.

2. We have a throw-away *society* where many products have a useful life of only a few minutes.

3. And despite the environmental movement, each of us *produces* 15 percent more garbage than we did in 1960.

4. *Industry* says it just gave consumers what they wanted.

5. It certainly doesn't *solve* the entire problem.

NOUN	VERB	ADJECTIVE
1. exception	_____	_____
2. society	_____	_____
3. _____	produces	_____
4. industry	_____	_____
5. _____	solve	_____

Postviewing

WHAT DO YOU THINK?

Write your answers to the following questions. Then discuss your answers with the class.

1. What have you learned from this video?

   _____

   _____

2. Do you know of any recycling centers or companies in the area where you are now living? If so, describe them. What sorts of materials do they collect?

   _____

   _____

3. Is trash a problem in your home culture? If so, what efforts are being made to solve the problem?

   _____

   _____

READING FOR INSIGHT

Read the article below, and then answer the comprehension and opinion questions that follow.

The Recycling Mapmaker

BRIGHT IDEA

Marianne Hegeman was a graduate student in the Geography Department of San Francisco State University when she thought up the idea of making a recycling map to meet the class project requirement of one of her professors. According to Ms. Hegeman, "People want to know visually where stores are located, and also what they sell. They never know where good secondhand stores or recycling centers are. Addresses are not enough."

LEGWORK

Ms. Hegeman decided to create a recycling map for the city of Albany, California. To get the information she needed, she had to do a lot of legwork. She went around to all the stores in the community and found out which ones bought and sold used goods. She also found out which ones specialized in specific items, such as old books. She included any store or facility that dealt with recycling or reuse.

TREASURE MAP

Her "Recycle and Reuse Map" not only shows where all the recycling facilities in Albany are located, it also shows where all the shops that buy and sell used items are. "Recycling is about more than just sorting your garbage; it's about reusing things that still have life in them," Ms. Hegeman says. At the bottom of her map, she provided the names, addresses and telephone numbers of all the stores and facilities shown on the map, along with a list of the items sold or collected by each.

IN THE NEWS

Ms. Hegeman gave the map to the Albany city officials. "They loved it," she says. The officials arranged for 5,000 copies to be printed and used the map as an insert in the city's quarterly newsletter to Albany residents. The map was also posted in local stores. After only one year, the "Recycle and Reuse Map" was so popular that the city had to do a second printing.

Adapted and reprinted with permission from *The Next Step: 50 More Things You Can Do to Save the Earth*, by the EarthWorks Group, 1991, Andrews and McMeel, p. 27.

COMPREHENSION QUESTIONS

1. How did Marianne Hegeman get the idea to make her map?

   _____

   _____

2. Why did she think that a recycling map would more helpful to people than a list of recycling shops and facilities? Do you agree with her reasoning? Why or why not?

   _____

   _____

3. How did she get the information she needed?

   _____

   _____

4. What information did she include about each store and facility shown on the map?

   _____

   _____

5. What did the Albany city officials do with the map?

   _____

   _____

IN YOUR OPINION

1. Would you be interested in having a recycle and reuse map of your own community? Why or why not?

   _____

   _____

2. Do you know of any other people who have thought up and carried out original ideas for improving the environment? If so, who are they and what did they do?

_____

_____

SPECIAL RESEARCH ASSIGNMENT

According to the news report on the video segment, a third of what Americans discard is merely packaging. How much aluminum, cardboard, cellophane, foil, paper, plastic and polystyrene foam is used to package the foods you buy? Visit a local grocery store or supermarket. See how many foods you can find with no wrapping, with one wrapping, with two wrappings, and with three or more wrappings. Use the chart below to list the foods you find. After you've finished, compare and discuss your findings in small groups. Then report your group's conclusions to the class.

FOODS WITH NO WRAPPING	FOODS WITH ONE WRAPPING
Example: whole watermelons	*Example: bread* (in a plastic or cellophane bag)
1. _____	1. _____
2. _____	2. _____
3. _____	3. _____
4. _____	4. _____
5. _____	5. _____
FOODS WITH TWO WRAPPINGS	**THREE OR MORE WRAPPINGS**
Example: corn flakes (in a cellophane bag inside a cardboard box)	*Example: microwavable noodles* (in a plastic cup covered with cellophane inside a cardboard box)
1. _____	1. _____
2. _____	2. _____
3. _____	3. _____
4. _____	4. _____
5. _____	5. _____

ROLE PLAY

You are a researcher for ABC News. Telephone your partner and ask the questions on the questionnaire. Your partner's book should be closed while you interview him or her. When you finish, your partner will interview you.

RECYCLING QUESTIONNAIRE

1. Do you regularly reuse or recycle any of the following items?
   (Answer yes, no, or do not use.)

		YES	NO	DO NOT USE
a.	aluminum cans	( )	( )	( )
b.	aluminum foil	( )	( )	( )
c.	cardboard boxes	( )	( )	( )
d.	computer paper	( )	( )	( )
e.	glass bottles and jars	( )	( )	( )
f.	plastic bottles	( )	( )	( )
g.	plastic food containers	( )	( )	( )
h.	plastic grocery bags	( )	( )	( )
i.	paper grocery bags	( )	( )	( )
j.	newspapers	( )	( )	( )
k.	magazines	( )	( )	( )

2. If you make a conscious effort to reuse or recycle, which one of the
   following statements best reflects your reason for doing so?
   a. I want to save money.
   b. I want to save energy and natural resources.
   c. I want to prevent pollution.
   d. I am concerned about the environment, and reusing or recycling is
      one way I can make a difference.

3. If you do not make a conscious effort to reuse or recycle, which one of
   the following statements best reflects your reason for not doing so?
   a. I haven't given reusing or recycling much thought.
   b. I don't have enough space to collect recyclables.
   c. It's too much trouble.
   d. I know the environment is in trouble, but I really don't care.

FINAL TASK: MAKE A RECYCLING MAP

Work in groups. Draw up a map of the recycling and reuse facilities in the
community where you are now living. Follow these steps:

1. Decide what area you want to include. Your map can cover the whole
   town or just one neighborhood, such as the immediate area around
   your school or college. Remember: the bigger the area, the more legwork
   you will have to do.

2. Decide what kinds of places you want to include. You may wish to limit your map to "official" recycling centers, or add places where secondhand goods are sold. For example: used book stores and flea markets.

3. Decide who will be responsible for visiting and obtaining information from the stores or recycling centers on particular streets, blocks, etc. You may find it easier and more enjoyable to do the actual legwork in pairs.

4. Visit stores and recycling centers in the area to be covered by your map. Find out what goods they accept, when they're open, etc. Note down the information and ask for permission to list the facilities on your map.

5. When your group meets again, draw up your map. Include the name, address, and phone number of each store or recycling center.

6. Present your map to the class and make a brief oral report on what your group found out about recycling and reuse facilities in the area covered by your map.

Segment 10

Solar Energy

from: *American Agenda*, 9/11/89
Runtime: 5:29
Begin: 45:50

Previewing

KEY QUESTIONS

1. How do solar energy systems work?
2. What are some uses of solar energy?
3. What are the advantages and disadvantages of solar energy over other energy sources?
4. How does the cost of solar energy compare with the cost of other sources of energy?

WHAT DO YOU ALREADY KNOW?

What do you already know about solar energy? Are the following statements true (*T*) or false (*F*)? The answers are on page 110.

_____ 1. Solar electricity is less expensive than power from coal or oil.
_____ 2. Solar electricity doesn't pollute the environment.
_____ 3. Solar water heaters are used in the White House in Washington, D.C.
_____ 4. Solar-powered vehicles are extremely efficient.
_____ 5. Cars powered by solar energy don't need to have their batteries recharged.

ESSENTIAL WORDS TO KNOW

The following words are used on the video. Read the sentences. Then match the words with their meanings.

barrel:	In 1989 the U.S. imported 7.9 million *barrels* of oil.
supertanker:	The *supertanker* had an accident off the Florida coast.
panel:	Solar *panels* are used to absorb sunlight.
recharge:	I need to *recharge* my car battery.

_____ 1. barrel
_____ 2. supertanker
_____ 3. panel
_____ 4. recharge

a. a board on which controls are fastened
b. (to cause) to take in more electricity
c. round container for liquid
d. ship for carrying large quantities of liquid

Global Viewing

46:04-
50:23

FIND THE MAIN IDEAS

Watch the video and circle the correct answer to each question.

1. According to Peter Jennings, what do some people in the U.S. think is a dangerous trend?
   a. Importing less oil and spending more money on research for other energy sources.
   b. Importing more oil and spending less money on research for other energy sources.
   c. Driving solar-powered cars and trucks.

2. What is the biggest advantage of solar power?
   a. It doesn't cost anything.
   b. It doesn't pollute the environment.
   c. It doesn't make any noise.

3. Why did James Worden drive cross-country in a solar-powered car?
   a. To prove that solar energy is practical.
   b. To win $10,000.
   c. To participate in the opening meeting of the U.S. Congress.

4. What is the biggest problem with solar energy?
   a. It is available only in Japan and Germany.
   b. It produces radioactivity.
   c. It is inefficient compared to other sources of energy.

Intensive Viewing

COMPLETE THE SENTENCES

Watch the part of the video that shows James Worden on the highway. Then complete the following sentences.

46:40-48:00

1. James Worden drove from _____ to _____ in a solar-powered car.

2. The large flat panel on James Worden's car absorbs _____ and converts it into _____ .

3. Solar electricity is about _____ times as costly as power from coal or oil.

4. Arco Solar, the company that financed James Worden's trip, is now owned by a _____ conglomerate (group of companies).

INFORMATION MATCH

Watch the rest of the video segment and match the information with the right name.

48:00-49:30

a. Scott Sklar
b. General Motors
c. William Rusnack
d. Jimmy Carter
e. Ronald Reagan
f. James Worden

_____ 1. This man thinks solar energy may not be cost-competitive.
_____ 2. This U.S. president put up solar heaters at the White House.
_____ 3. This man hopes to market a solar-powered car for $10,000.
_____ 4. This man was the U. S. president when the solar panels were removed from the White House.
_____ 5. This company built a solar-powered car called the Sun Raycer.
_____ 6. This man is worried that the U.S. will have to import electric cars from overseas.

LISTENING CLOZE

The passages below are from the video. Watch the video again and fill in the blanks with the missing words.

46:03-46:28

Passage 1

Peter Jennings: Tonight we have put the subject of solar power on the *American Agenda* and here is why. Consider this: in _____ the U.S. imported _____ million barrels of foreign oil and spent _____ million dollars on research into other renewable sources of energy. This year the U.S. will import _____ million barrels of foreign oil and spend _____ million dollars on research for other energy sources.

111

Passage 2

47:25-
47:43 **Ned Potter**: Solar panels are still terribly _____ , and
that makes solar electricity five times as costly as the power from coal or
oil. But there is no _____ to the environment. It does not foul the
air, cause radioactive _____ , or spill from supertankers.

Passage 3

48:47-
49:23 **Ned Potter**: Carter was wrong. The _____ came down in the
Reagan years when OPEC _____ began flowing more cheaply. Most of
the tax breaks expired, research money for solar dried up. And giant
_____ like Shell, Westinghouse and Exxon lost interest. James
Worden drove cross-country to _____ solar practical. He hopes to
market a commuter car soon for $10,000. But General Motors won't put
a price _____ on its car, the Sun Raycer. G.M. says solar cells are still
too inefficient for anything but an _____ .

Language Focus

GETTING THE MEANING FROM CONTEXT

46:50-
50:23 Listen to the following passages from the video transcript. Try to define the
meaning of the *italicized* words and expressions from the context of the
sentence.

James Worden: And our message is that if we can cross the country, 3,000
miles, *by golly*, everyone can drive to work and back in a solar electric car.

1. *By golly* is an informal way of expressing _____ .
   a. surprise or wonder
   b. sorrow or disappointment

Ned Potter: Will the U.S. *stick with* it? Solar panels are ten times more
efficient than a decade ago, and companies say they'll be *in the black* by the
mid-1990s. But until then they need some *backing*.

2. When you *stick with* something, you _____ .
   a. don't quit
   b. stop doing it

3. When a company is *in the black*, it is _____ .
   a. losing money
   b. making a profit

112

4. *Backing* means _____ .
   a. help or support
   b. advertising

Ned Potter: James Worden pulled up at the Capitol on a *blazing* morning and *showed off* his car to members of Congress.

James Worden: Yea! We *made it.*

5. A *blazing* morning is _____ .
   a. bright and warm
   b. dark and cold

6. When you *show off* something, you _____ .
   a. display it to other people
   b. remove it

7. In the context above, *made it* means _____ .
   a. arrived
   b. built or constructed it

Peter Jennings: It may take as long as 12 hours to recharge the car's batteries. *Mind you*, it is an experimental car.

8. *Mind you* is an informal way of telling someone to _____ .
   a. understand
   b. obey

WORD FORMS

The sentences below are from the video segment. The words in italics are either nouns, verbs or adjectives. Complete the grid below by adding the other forms of the *italicized* word. When you finish compare your chart with that of another student.

1. Consider this: in 1980 the U.S. imported 6.8 million barrels of foreign oil and spent $600 million on research into other *renewable* sources of energy.

2. It's a *hazy* morning over Los Angeles.

3. All this *power* comes from above, from sunlight absorbed by that large flat panel on top and converted to electricity.

4. We see solar energy having a very difficult time being cost-*competitive* as a source of primary energy for the United States and the rest of the world.

5. Meanwhile, *analysts* say the Germans and the Japanese blaze the trail, because their governments are spending more than ours and their corporations are often more patient for profits.

6. Back then, President Carter ordered research money and tax breaks for any good *alternative* petroleum.

7. In the year 2000, this solar heater behind me which is being *dedicated* today will still be here.

8. GM says solar cells are still too inefficient for anything but an *experiment*.

NOUN	VERB	ADJECTIVE
1. _____	_____	renewable
2. _____	_____	hazy
3. power	_____	_____
4. _____	_____	competitive
5. analysts	_____	_____
6. _____	_____	alternative
7. _____	dedicated	_____
8. experiment	_____	_____

Postviewing

WHAT DO YOU THINK?

Write your answers to the following questions. Then work in small groups and discuss your answers.

1. Would you consider buying a solar-powered car? Why or why not?

_____

_____

2. What kind of people might buy a solar-powered car?

_____

_____

3. James Worden said that if he could cross the country by solar power, "everyone can drive to work and back in a solar electric car." Do you agree with him? Why or why not?

_____

_____

RELATED READING: SUCCESS WITH SOLAR COOKING

Read the article below and then answer the questions that follow.

Cooking with the Sun

Imagine cooking a beef roast with all the fixings in a cardboard box. Cindy Kuehl of Mechanicsville, Iowa, did. "And it worked great," she said.

Ms. Kuehl became fascinated by solar cookers after seeing a demonstration on television in June 1989. She wanted to build one herself so she called her state energy office for help and was referred to the National Appropriate Technology Assistance Service (NATAS) in Butte, Montana, for help. Her case was assigned to Information Specialist Jim Masker who sent her descriptions and plans for three different solar cookers.

Ms. Kuehl, a frugal homemaker who enjoys doing "craft things," elected to build the least expensive cooker. She found a heavy cardboard box at a local machinery dealership and bought a pane of glass for the top of the cooker. She rummaged around her house for the rest of the materials—glue, black paint, newspapers, and contact paper. "The only thing I had to pay for was the piece of glass," she said. Using plans Masker sent, she went to work assembling her cooker. "It took four to five hours to make," Ms. Kuehl said.

Roasts and other dishes she has cooked in her solar oven have taken a while longer—the pot roast, for instance. Early in the morning, she placed it in a pot and tucked vegetables around it. Then she forgot about it except to turn the box occasionally toward the sun throughout the day. By dinner time, the roast was done and her kitchen was still cool.

Ms. Kuehl has used the cooker to bake apples and roast other meat and vegetable dishes. She doesn't use it every day, of course, and she doesn't use it for every meal. "It has to be a hot, sunny day for it to work," she said. "If it's a little cloudy, it doesn't work well."

Still, on an Iowa summer day, a solar cooker can save energy.

And now Ms. Kuehl is wondering how solar-baked cookies and bread would taste.

Reprinted with permission from *Success Stories, National Appropriate Technology Assistance Service,* [n.d.], United States Department of Energy, p. 6.

COMPREHENSION QUESTIONS

1. Who is Cindy Kuehl?

   _____

   _____

2. How did she become interested in solar cookers?

   _____

   _____

3. What organization provided her with plans for building a solar cooker?

   _____

   _____

4. What materials did she use to build it?

   _____

   _____

5. How long did it take her to build it?

   _____

   _____

6. How long did it take her to cook a pot roast in it?

   _____

   _____

7. What are some other things has she already cooked in her solar oven?

   _____

   _____

8. Why doesn't she use her solar oven every day?

   _____

   _____

RELATED READING: SOLAR HOMES

Read the article *Some Questions and Answers About Solar Homes* and complete the checklist that follows.

Some Questions and Answers About Solar Homes

The president of the United States may not live in a solar home, but about a million other Americans do. For the most part, they are happy with their solar heating systems, and many have become enthusiastic supporters of solar energy. Here are answers to some of the questions most frequently asked about solar energy systems.

Q. How do solar energy systems work?

A. Solar radiation is absorbed by collectors and placed in storage. The stored heat is then distributed to the rooms of the house. Manual or automatic controls are used to run the collection and storage operations.

Q. What kinds of solar energy systems are there?

A. There are two basic types of solar energy systems: active and passive. Active systems use pumps and pipes (or fans and ducts) to carry heat from the collectors to storage, and from storage to the rooms of the house. Passive systems make use of large windows to collect the heat, and thick walls and floors to store the heat for later use.

Q. How are solar homes heated at night?

A. With an active system, the heat generated all day in the collectors has been transferred to the storage system. At night, this heat is circulated from storage to the rooms of the house. In a well-designed passive building, enough heat can be stored to keep it warm through the night.

Q. What happens if there are a few cloudy or cold days in a row?

A. After the heat in an active system is used up, an auxiliary system takes over. Any standard oil, electricity, coal or gas system may be used. In a passive system, the storage components can absorb enough heat to last through a day or two of sunless weather. After that, an auxiliary heater is used. Many passive homeowners say that a wood stove gives them all the backup heat they need.

Q. Can a solar energy system produce air conditioning?

A. An active solar energy system can be used to drive an absorption air conditioner, but these systems are more expensive than conventional air conditioning systems. Homes can also be designed to incorporate inexpensive and efficient passive solar air conditioning systems, but such systems work best in climates with low humidity and cool nights. However, basic passive cooling techniques such as shading windows are effective and can be used anywhere.

Are the following sentences about active solar energy systems, passive solar energy systems, or both active and passive solar energy systems? Check (✓) the appropriate column.

	Active Systems	Passive Systems	Both Systems
1. They make use of controls to run the collection and storage systems.	_____	_____	_____
2. They use large windows for heat collection and thick walls and floors for storage.	_____	_____	_____
3. They may use pumps and pipes to carry heat from collectors to storage.	_____	_____	_____
4. They store heat collected during the day for use at night.	_____	_____	_____
5. They make use of backup heating systems when stored heat is used up.	_____	_____	_____
6. They can be used to drive efficient, inexpensive air conditioning systems.	_____	_____	_____
7. They can be used to drive absorption air conditioners.	_____	_____	_____
8. They can be used in conjunction with basic passive cooling techniques.	_____	_____	_____

ROLE PLAY

For this role play, a student volunteer will play the role of James Worden. The rest of the class will play the roles of reporters. Read the situation and role descriptions below, decide who will play James Worden, and after a ten-minute preparation, begin the press conference.

The Situation: A Press Conference

James Worden, "the Henry Ford of the environmental age," has just completed his 3,000 mile trip across the United States in his solar electric car. Today he will be interviewed by a group of reporters at his hotel in Washington, D.C.

ROLE DESCRIPTION: JAMES WORDEN

You strongly believe that solar electric cars are a practical alternative to gas driven vehicles. In your opinion, everyone should consider buying one. Think about the questions the reporters will probably ask you at the press conference. Be prepared to answer them.

ROLE DESCRIPTION: REPORTERS

You are a reporter representing a television or radio station, a newspaper, or a magazine from another country. Make up a list of at least five questions to ask James Worden: about himself, his solar electric car, his reasons for making his trip, and anything else that is relevant.

WRITE A NEWSPAPER ARTICLE

Write your own news report about James Worden's trip from Los Angeles to Washington, D.C. In your report, be sure to answer the six question words: Who? What? Where? When? Why? and How?

FINAL TASK: CONDUCT A SURVEY

1. Work in groups and write a questionnaire. Make up five yes/no questions to find out people's opinions about solar energy. Your group will interview a cross-section of people. Decide when and where you will conduct the survey, how many people you will question, who they will be, etc. When you take the survey, count the yes and no responses. Take notes on the interesting comments that people make. The following grid can be used to write your questions, count responses, and record comments.

Questions	Yes	No	Comments
Example: Would you consider buying a solar-powered car?	//	###	I wouldn't know where to go to buy one.
1.			
2.			
3.			
4.			
5.			

2. When your group meets again, summarize the information you have collected and prepare an oral report to present to the class. Be sure to include an introduction to your survey, a summary of the results, and a conclusion. The conclusion should include your group's interpretation of the information collected.

3. When you present your oral reports to the class, follow this procedure:
   a. One student introduces the group and gives an introduction to the survey conducted by the group.
   b. The next few students present one or two of the questions, statistics on yes and no responses, and some interesting comments made by the people who were interviewed.
   c. The last student concludes the presentation by summarizing and interpreting the information, and perhaps reacting to the results; e.g.,"It surprised us to learn that most people . . ."

Segment 11

A Look at European Mass Transit

from: *American Agenda*, 6/6/90
Runtime: 5:05
Begin: 50:42

Previewing

KEY QUESTIONS

1. What substitutes have Europeans developed for the car?
2. How do these substitutes protect the environment?
3. What can Americans learn from European approaches to mass transit?

DISCUSSION

1. What different forms of transportation are available in your city?

   _____

   _____

2. How many of these forms of transportation have you traveled on?

   _____

   _____

3. What forms of transportation do you take to get from your home to your school or college?

   _____

   _____

PREDICTION

Based on the title of the segment, *A Look at European Mass Transit*, and the picture above, what information do you think will be included on the video?

1. _____

2. _____

3. _____

ESSENTIAL WORDS TO KNOW

The following words are used on the video. Read the sentences below. Then match the words with their meanings.

carbon monoxide:	Coal mine explosions produce *carbon monoxide*.
autobahn:	We drove on the *autobahn* from Hamburg to Bremen.
smog:	A layer of *smog* hung over the city.
pollute:	Gasoline fumes *pollute* the city air.
gridlock:	How can we reduce *gridlock* during rush hours?
detour:	They made a *detour* around the city center.

_____ 1. carbon monoxide
_____ 2. autobahn
_____ 3. smog
_____ 4. pollute
_____ 5. gridlock
_____ 6. detour

a. to contaminate, to make dirty
b. a colorless, odorless, poisonous gas
c. continuous lines of traffic that cannot move
d. a superhighway in Germany
e. a route used when the main road is blocked
f. a mixture of fog, smoke, and gases in the air

Global Viewing

FIND THE MAIN IDEAS

51:00-
55:30

Read the following sentences. Then watch the video and check (✓) the sentences that are *true*. Compare your answers with those of another student. If you disagree, watch the video again.

_____ 1. Congestion and pollution are serious problems in European and American cities.

_____ 2. Europeans are developing substitutes for the car.

_____ 3. Americans are more willing than Europeans to pay the cost of developing substitutes for the car.

_____ 4. Big budget plans to develop substitutes for the car are common in the United States.

_____ 5. Advanced technology is necessary to make mass transit work.

_____ 6. The Europeans interviewed on the video are unhappy with the results of the new transportation plans.

_____ 7. The car needs to be eliminated in order to solve mass transit problems in the United States.

Intensive Viewing

USEFUL WORDS AND PHRASES

Before watching the first part of the video again, look at these sentences spoken by Peter Jennings. Which of the words and phrases below belong in spaces 1–6? Write them in. The first one has been done for you. Then watch the video again and check your answers.

51:00-
51:21

aggressively	congestion	the world's favorite people mover ✓
civilized	its own way	willing to pay

In Europe, as in the U.S., (1) <u>the world's favorite people mover</u> is getting in (2) _____ . The automobile is creating (3) _____ and pollution wherever it goes, but unlike Americans, Europeans are moving (4) _____ to develop some (5) _____ substitutes for the car. The biggest difference in approach may be simply that Europe is (6) _____ the price.

GETTING THE FACTS

Watch the scene in Paris again. Choose the correct answer to each question.

51:28-
51:40

1. What's the average speed of traffic coming into Paris each morning?
   a. 6 miles an hour.
   b. 16 miles an hour.
   c. 60 miles an hour.

2. How many people drive into Paris each day?
   a. 1 million
   b. 1.3 million
   c. 3 million.

3. How many times the safety level are carbon monoxide levels in Paris?
   a. Two.
   b. Three.
   c. Four.

INFORMATION MATCH

52:15-53:40

Watch the scenes in Germany and match the information in the column on the right to the kinds of vehicles in the column on the left. Write the letters in the correct boxes below each vehicle. There are several answers for each vehicle. Some letters can be used more than once.

Vehicles used in Germany

1. Diesel buses in Essen

☐ ☐ ☐ ☐ ☐

2. Maglevs in Berlin

☐ ☐ ☐ ☐ ☐

3. Trolleys in Karlsruhe

☐ ☐ ☐ ☐ ☐

These vehicles...

a. have no engine
b. cost a billion dollars to build
c. travel on streets
d. protect the environment
e. transform themselves into electric trolleys
f. float on magnets
g. can go anywhere in the suburbs
h. are preferred to cars by 75% of the people
i. are a U.S. invention
j. have wheels
k. arrive every 50 seconds

TRUE OR FALSE?

53:50-54:25

Read the sentences below. Then watch the scenes in Holland. As you watch, decide whether each statement is true or false. Write *T* or *F*.

_____ 1. The Dutch government has tried to make bicycling more attractive to people.

_____ 2. There are bicycle lanes on the major streets in Holland.

_____ 3. Parking lots in shopping centers in Holland are reserved for bicycles.

_____ 4. Cars cannot get downtown in the city of Delft.

_____ 5. Bicycling increased in Holland as a result of the government's plan.

_____ 6. Dutch people make a third of all their trips by bicycle.

NOTETAKING

54:35-55:30

Read the following questions. Then watch the last part of the video and make brief notes on the answers. Compare your answers with those of another student. If you disagree, watch the video again.

1. Why is it easier to make changes in mass transit in Western Europe?

_____

_____

2. How much is the average gas tax in the U.S.? How much is it in Europe?

_____

_____

3. Why do European governments think gas taxes will have to rise more?

_____

_____

4. In addition to clean air, what are some other payoffs (positive results) of finding alternatives to the car?

_____

_____

5. According to Ned Potter, what is the "message for . . . Americans"?

_____

_____

Language Focus

GETTING THE MEANING FROM CONTEXT

Read these passages from the video, paying special attention to the *italicized* words and expressions. Select the best synonym for each.

So European governments have started something almost unseen in America: *comprehensive* big budget plans to give people *appealing* alternatives to their cars.

1. *comprehensive*:
   a. simple
   b. complete
   c. incomplete
   d. hard to understand

2. *appealing*:
   a. boring
   b. expensive
   c. attractive
   d. useless

It can go anywhere in the *suburbs*. It *outsmarts* downtown traffic and cuts *urban* smog.

3. *suburbs*:
   a. shopping areas
   b. residential areas close to a large city
   c. residential areas in a large city
   d. residential areas far from a large city

4. *outsmarts*:
   a. acts more clever than
   b. goes slower than
   c. eliminates
   d. increases

5. *urban*:
   a. caused by engines
   b. caused by factories
   c. in a city
   d. in the country

Then a *transmitter* turns the lights green.

6. *transmitter*:
   a. something that sends a signal
   b. something that pulls a car
   c. someone who drives a car
   d. someone who guards the road

Karlsruhe, West Germany, has a traditional trolley *network* which is so *extensive* that 75 percent of the people prefer it to their cars.

7. *network*:
   a. connected system
   b. parking lot
   c. engine
   d. branch

8. *extensive*:
   a. small in area
   b. large in area
   c. costing a lot of money
   d. costing a little money

But high as those prices are, Europeans say they will have to rise much more—perhaps double—to *steer people away* from the habits that endanger the planet.

9. *steer people away*:
   a. get people to start
   b. get people to remember
   c. encourage people to avoid
   d. encourage people to use

Europeans say the *payoffs* go beyond clean air. They can mean a better lifestyle in general.

10. *payoffs*:
   a. money lost
   b. benefits
   c. money won
   d. money paid

WORD PUZZLE

Complete the puzzle by answering the down clues. All of the words are used in the video segment. The keyword is "the world's favorite people mover".

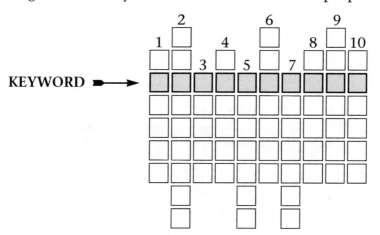

Clues
1. _____ monoxide is poisonous.
2. a broad street, often with trees on either side
3. money paid to the government
4. Ned _____ is a reporter for ABC News.
5. A maglev floats on _____ .
6. an electric streetcar
7. Germany spent a _____ dollars to build a maglev system.
8. a type of oil-burning engine often used in trucks, buses, and trains
9. another name for the Netherlands
10. large city in Germany

Postviewing

WHAT DO YOU THINK?

Write your answers to the following questions. Then discuss your answers in groups.

1. Which of the mass transit plans described on the video might be useful in your city?

   _____

   _____

2. Which plan would be the most difficult to put into use? Why?

   _____

   _____

3. Which plan is most appealing to you? Why?

   _____

   _____

RELATED READING: THE MAGLEV

Read the article *The Maglev Takes Off* to learn more about: (1) how the maglev works, (2) the history of the maglev, and (3) interest in the maglev in the U.S. and in other countries. Then fill in the notetaking form that follows.

The Maglev Takes Off

The maglev has been called "the flying train." Driven by magnetic forces, it floats above a guideway at a speed of 300 miles an hour. Will Americans soon be riding maglevs? Maybe, but the first maglev systems in the U.S. will probably be built by Germany or Japan, even though the technology was invented in the U.S.

The first maglev was developed in the early '70s by physicist Henry Kolm and engineer Richard Thornton at the Massachusetts Institute of Technology. The inventors ran their 40-inch scale model, which they called the Magneplane, down a 400-foot test track hundreds of times before funding for the magneplane project was cut off.

As Americans become more concerned about air pollution and traffic congestion, interest in the maglev is picking up speed. A National Maglev Institute has been created to coordinate efforts by the U.S. Departments of Transportation and Energy, the Federal Railroad Administration, and private industry, and U.S. senators are asking for more money for maglev-related projects. President George Bush asked for $9.7 million in the 1991 budget to study the maglev.

However, U.S. industry remains skeptical about how serious the government is and how long investments in the maglev will take to pay off. Meanwhile, Germany and Japan are speeding ahead in their efforts to export the maglev. Russia has already agreed to buy maglev technology from the Japanese. Within a few years, Japanese maglevs will be carrying Russians from downtown Moscow to the airport.

In the United States, a German-built maglev system is being considered for the 250-mile route between Los Angeles and Las Vegas. However, the German maglev faces strong competition from the TVG, a French-built turbo-electric train which travels at the same speed. Whether or not the Germans win that race, German-built maglevs may be put into use in Florida. These maglevs, which would speed tourists from the Orlando airport to Disney World, would not be financed by Americans, but by Japanese banks.

Because of the maglev's low energy needs and its minimal impact on the land, environmentalists feel it is an appealing alternative to other mass transit systems. However, if the flying train is to become widely used in the U.S., American business will have to show more interest in getting involved.

  I. How the maglev works

    A. Speed at which it travels: _____

    B. Forces which drive it: _____

 II. History of the maglev

    A. Inventors:

       1. _____

       2. _____

    B. Where developed: _____

    C. When developed: _____

    D. Size of the model: _____

    E. Length of the test track: _____

III. Facts that suggest U.S. interest in the maglev is increasing:

    A. _____

    B. _____

    C. _____

IV. Reasons U.S. industry has been slow to invest in the maglev:

    A. _____

    B. _____

  V. Worldwide interest in the maglev

    A. Countries that are trying to export the maglev:

       1. _____

       2. _____

VI. Reasons the maglev appeals to people who are concerned about the environment:

A. _____

B. _____

RELATED READING: HOW TO MAKE CYCLING CONVENIENT

Read the article *Seven Ways to Make Cycling More Convenient* and answer the questions that follow.

Seven Ways to Make Cycling More Convenient

Americans make only 0.5% of their trips by bicycle. If they made only 2% more of their trips by bike, carbon monoxide levels would go down 5%.

"The only way to get people to ride bicycles instead of cars is to make cycling more convenient," says Julie Falsetti, president of "Bike Buddies," a club for New York City residents who cycle to work. How can cycling be made more convenient? Here are seven ideas from around the world.

1. Provide Safe Cycling Routes. In Cambridge, England, a bike "tube" has been built over a large railroad area. In Denmark, bike underpasses have been built under highways to provide safer cycling routes.

2. End Free Parking. In Japan and in European countries where cycling to work is common, parking is expensive or unavailable. By contrast, in the U.S., 75% of all commuters have a free parking space at work. If free parking were eliminated, car use could decrease by 25%.

3. Make Sunday "Bike Day." Every Sunday 30 miles of city streets in Bogota, Colombia, are closed to cars. This increases cycling and reduces pollution.

4. Give Tax Breaks. In Holland, the government records each car's mileage. Low-mileage drivers pay lower taxes. This results in a lot less driving.

5. Set up Car Barriers. In some German cities, car barriers are placed every two or three blocks. By closing off car traffic, safer routes are created for cyclists.

6. Charge Congestion Tolls. In Singapore, cars with fewer than four passengers have to pay a "congestion fee" during rush hours. If drivers had to pay a fee for driving alone, the money collected could be used for mass transit and bike-related projects.

7. Establish Alternate Driving Days. In Santiago, Chile, and Milan, Italy, a license plate code system is used to keep 20% of all motor vehicles off the road on any given day. This encourages cycling and car pooling.

IN YOUR OPINION

1. Which ideas for making cycling more convenient seem most practical to you? Why?

_____

_____

2. Which ideas, if any, would be impractical in your home culture? Why?

_____

_____

3. What ideas do you have for making cycling more convenient where you live now?

_____

_____

IDENTIFYING FACTUAL ERRORS

The notes below are based on the article *Seven Ways to Make Cycling More Convenient*. Four of them contain factual errors. Compare the notes with the information in the article and make the necessary corrections.

1. If Americans took 20% more trips by bike, carbon monoxide levels would be reduced by 5%.
2. Parking is expensive or unavailable in Japan and in some European countries.
3. Free parking space is available to most Americans who drive to work.
4. Thirty miles of the city streets in Bogota, Colombia, are closed to motor vehicles on Saturdays.
5. In Holland, each car's mileage is recorded, and low-mileage drivers pay higher taxes.
6. In some German cities, car barriers are used to close off car traffic.
7. Cars with more than four passengers pay a "congestion fee" during rush hours in Singapore.
8. The license plate code system in Santiago, Chile, reduces cycling and car pooling.

ROLE PLAY

You are a researcher for ABC News. Telephone your partner and ask the questions on the questionnaire. Your partner's book should be closed while you interview him or her. When you finish, your partner will interview you.

MASS TRANSIT QUESTIONNAIRE

1. On an average day, how many trips do you make by mass transit? _____
2. How many trips did you make yesterday? _____
3. What form(s) of mass transit did you take yesterday? _____
4. What is your favorite form of mass transit? _____

5. Do you agree or disagree with the following statements about the mass transit system in your city or town?

	AGREE	DISAGREE	DON'T KNOW
a. The mass transit fares are too expensive.	( )	( )	( )
b. The system is not extensive enough.	( )	( )	( )
c. The system is too slow.	( )	( )	( )
d. The conductors and drivers are rude.	( )	( )	( )
e. The system is always breaking down.	( )	( )	( )
f. The system causes too much pollution.	( )	( )	( )

FINAL TASK: WRITE A LETTER

Here are some complaints people have made about mass transit systems in their cities and towns.

The subway cars are too noisy.
The trolley seats are uncomfortable.
The buses are too crowded.
The subway stations are dirty.

What is the biggest problem with the mass transit system where you live? Write a letter to the mayor of your city or town. Describe the problem and suggest a solution.

Segment 12

Environmental Concerns Cause Shopper Discretion

from: *American Agenda*, 1/23/90
Runtime: 4:50
Begin: 55:51

Previewing

KEY QUESTIONS

1. What does the term "green consumerism" mean?
2. How can you tell which products are environmentally safe?
3. What can be done to encourage companies to make their products environmentally safe?

DISCUSSION

1. Do you base any of your shopping decisions on how they will affect the environment? Which ones?

   _____

   _____

2. How do you decide whether a product is environmentally safe?

   _____

   _____

PREDICTION

Based on the title of the segment *Environmental Concerns Cause Shopper Discretion* and your own background knowledge, what information do you think will be included in the video segment?

1. _____

2. _____

3. _____

4. _____

ESSENTIAL WORDS TO KNOW

Look at the following sentences. The *italicized* words are used in the video segment. Match the words with the definitions below.

a. to throw away
b. a trick that is used to attract attention
c. to blame or accuse
d. to refuse to buy

e. a style or tendency that others follow
f. someone who sells things to the general public

_____ 1. What is the latest *trend* in women's clothes?

_____ 2. Environmental groups often *target* manufacturers for the pollution they cause.

_____ 3. Shoppers may *boycott* a product for environmental reasons.

_____ 4. That *retailer* has gone out of business.

_____ 5. Americans *discard* two and half million plastic bottles every hour.

_____ 6. Is green consumerism a public relations *gimmick*?

Global Viewing

FIND THE MAIN IDEAS

56:04-
1:00:35

Read the following sentences. Then watch the video and check the sentences that are *true*. Compare your answers with those of another student. If you disagree, watch the video again.

_____ 1. Green consumerism is a rapidly developing trend in the United States.

_____ 2. A majority of Americans say they are concerned about the environmental effects of the products they buy.

_____ 3. Some companies in the United States are attempting to meet consumer demands for environmentally safe products.

_____ 4. Green consumerism is already a powerful political force in Europe.

_____ 5. American companies say that they will join the green consumer trend whether or not they make money at it.

_____ 6. When a product is labeled "environmentally safe," you can be sure that is has been tested and proved safe for the environment.

CONFIRMING YOUR PREDICTIONS

Watch the entire video segment. As you watch, put a check (✓) next to any of your predictions from the previewing section that were mentioned.

56:04-
1:00:35

Prediction 1 _____   Prediction 3 _____

Prediction 2 _____   Prediction 4 _____

Intensive Viewing

LISTENING CLOZE

The passage below is the first part of the video transcript. View the first part of the video again and fill in the blanks with the missing words.

56:04-
57:05

Peter Jennings: We have put shopping on the American Agenda tonight. It doesn't _____ to all of us all the time, by any means, but whenever we buy almost anything in the _____ , we are making a decision about the environment, often an unconscious decision. We put this subject on the Agenda because in _____ of Europe and in Canada many people have been shopping for a very long time with the environment specifically in mind. Is there a _____ here? Here's ABC's Ned Potter.

Ned Potter: Every time you buy a burger, a diaper, detergent, mushrooms, or trash bags—in fact, every time you open your _____ —you make a choice that affects the _____ .

Woman: If there's anything that will help the _____ , I'm all for it.

Ned Potter: And if you agree with that feeling, you are already part of a _____ . Some call it "green consumerism," people basing their buying decisions on how they _____ the environment. The movement is still in its infancy, but few _____ in the U.S. economy are developing as quickly.

LISTENING FOR DETAILS

Watch the next part of the video. Circle the answers to these questions.

57:05-
57:20

1. What three environmental problems does Joel Makower mention?
   a. Acid rain, ocean pollution, endangered animals.
   b. The rain forest, ocean pollution, landfills.
   c. Acid rain, the ozone layer, landfills.

2. On what level does he say people can do a lot to solve these problems?
   a. On the personal level.
   b. On the corporate level.
   c. On the government level.

NOTETAKING

Watch the next part of the video and fill in the notetaking form below.

57:30-
58:05

1. Product environmental records:
   a. product with the worst rating: _____
   b. product with the best rating: _____
2. American interest in green consumerism:
   a. Percentage of Americans who are concerned about the environmental effects of the things they buy: _____
   b. Percentage of Americans who would pay more for items in recyclable packages: _____
   c. Percentage of Americans who have boycotted products for environmental reasons: _____

INFORMATION MATCH

Watch the next part of the video. Match the information below with the right place.

58:13-
59:52

a. England   e. Washington, D.C.
b. Arkansas   f. Seattle
c. Canada   g. New England
d. Germany   h. Europe

_____ 1. city in which Procter and Gamble is selling fabric softener in cartons instead of bottles
_____ 2. city in which people are trying to recycle disposable diapers
_____ 3. state where Wal-Mart has put green labels on environmentally safe products
_____ 4. region where McDonald's allows customers to separate their trash for recycling
_____ 5. country where Loblaw's launched a successful line of green products
_____ 6. continent where green consumerism has become a powerful political force
_____ 7. country that has a national seal of approval environmentally safe products
_____ 8. country in which cosmetics are promoted for how they help the earth

LISTENING FOR DETAILS

Watch the end of the video segment—more than once if you need to—and give brief answers to the questions below.

1. What do some companies do instead of improving their products?

   _____

   _____

2. What is Jeanne Wirka's opinion of some "environmentally friendly" products?

   _____

   _____

3. What "weapon" can consumers use to make business do the right thing for the environment?

   _____

   _____

Language Focus

VOCABULARY CHECK

The following excerpts are from the video segment. Match the *italicized* words and expressions with their equivalents below.

a. began to sell
b. official mark of a government, company, etc.
c. early period of development

d. exactly
e. short lived interest or practice
f. described

_____ 1. The movement is still in its *infancy*, but few trends in the U.S. economy are developing as quickly.

_____ 2. This is not going to be a *fad*.

_____ 3. David Nichol is president of Loblaw's, a Canadian supermarket giant that *launched* a line of green products so successful it forced other brands to imitate them.

_____ 4. Many products that are being *touted* as environmentally friendly are not.

_____ 5. Joel Makower is author of "The Green Consumer Guide," which tells consumers *specifically* what is good or bad to buy.

_____ 6. In West Germany, there is now a national *seal* of environmental approval for products.

USEFUL EXPRESSIONS

The sentences below are all spoken on the video. Circle the meaning of the *italicized* expressions.

1. If there's anything that will help the environment, *I'm all for it.*
   a. I'm completely in favor of it.
   b. I'm completely opposed to it.

2. People, I think, are pretty frustrated in not being able to solve acid rain or help *patch up* the ozone layer.
   a. mend the holes in
   b. reduce the size of

3. This is not a *fringe movement.*
   a. movement supported by a small number of people
   b. movement supported by a large number of people

4. If it is, OK, *I'll plead guilty to that*, but we're still doing good.
   a. I'll deny that.
   b. I'll admit that.

5. If companies do not *gear up* now, many of them fear they will be far behind the demands of the public.
   a. adapt to the situation
   b. ignore the situation

6. I realize that if a retailer does not *take those environmental concerns into account* today, they may not be in business tomorrow.
   a. make a profit from those environmental concerns
   b. consider those environmental concerns

7. American companies say *right up front* that if they are going to join the trend they will have to make money at it.
   a. secretly
   b. honestly

8. On the other hand, some of them might find it easier just to *slap on a new label* than actually improve the product.
   a. attach a new label carelessly
   b. attach a new label carefully

WORD PUZZLE

Find 10 words in the puzzle that match the definitions below. Draw a ring around each word as you find it, as in the example. The words can be in any direction—forward, backward, up, down, or diagonal. You can use letters more than once, but no word is inside another word. All the words are used on the video.

1. chemical product used for cleaning ✓
2. small flat case for holding money
3. fruit-flavored drink
4. edible, fungus-type plants
5. slip of paper attached to something to show what it is
6. boxes made from stiff paper
7. soft cloth or paper garment worn by babies
8. thin paper or plastic tubes for sucking up liquid
9. paper or cloth item used when eating
10. container for liquids, usually made of glass or plastic

Postviewing

READING FOR INSIGHT

Read the following excerpt from *Shopping for a Better World*. Your task is to:

1. Read the comprehension and opinion questions that follow the article to guide your reading.
2. Read the article quickly for main ideas and important points. Ignore words you do not understand.
3. Discuss your answers to the questions with other students.

Shopping for Better Packaging

Americans love packaging. And the products on supermarket and drugstore shelves reflect that love affair; nearly everything, it seems, is wrapped in something, sometimes a lot of things. Even produce—tomatoes and corn-on-the-cob, for example—sit neatly on a plastic foam tray, encased in clear plastic wrap. Some products have layers upon layers of packaging, for no apparent reason.

Some of that packaging is important—it prevents tampering, ensures cleanliness, and can be imprinted with helpful information, among another things. But a great deal of it is unnecessary and wasteful. You needn't walk far down any supermarket aisle to find a plastic bowl covered with a plastic lid, contained in a cardboard box, which is shrink-wrapped in yet more plastic. Ironically, some of these overpackaged goods are given awards by the packaging industry for their innovative designs. It is precisely these "innovations" that contribute to our clogged landfills. Of the roughly two tons of trash discarded by the average American each year, packaging accounts for an estimated 30%, or about 1,200 pounds a year for every man, woman, and child.

The problem isn't just the amount of packaging, it's also the type of materials being used. A growing number of products are being wrapped in "composites"— packages containing several layers of materials and adhesives, such as juice boxes, which contain layers of polyethylene, paperboard, and aluminum. Squeezable ketchup and mustard, made of up to seven layers of plastic and adhesives, are another example. The components of these materials cannot be separated from each other before being thrown away and cannot currently be recycled. These packages will end up in landfills, where they may take centuries to break down.

Even when packaging consists of only one type of material, it is often an unrecyclable one. The vast majority of Americans have no means to recycle most types of plastic or polystyrene, or even the kind of coated paperboard used in many product packages. Many manufacturers, attempting to lure environmentally conscious consumers, are labeling their packages "recyclable." That may be technically true—given the right technology and enough financing, the package could be recycled. But for now, glass, aluminum, steel, and corrugated cardboard are the only packaging materials easily recyclable.

Reprinted with permission from *Shopping for a Better World*, by The Council on Economic Priorities, 1990, Ballantine Books, pp. 271–272.

COMPREHENSION QUESTIONS

1. How many pounds of packaging does the average American discard each year?

_____

_____

2. What are "composites," and why are they a problem?

_____

_____

3. What is the problem with many packages that are labeled "recyclable"?

_____

_____

4. According to the article, what materials are easy to recycle?

_____

_____

IN YOUR OPINION

1. Why do you think Americans are so fond of packaging?

_____

_____

2. Do you think the packaging industry should continue to give awards for "innovations" in packaging? Why or why not?

_____

_____

3. Can you think of any products, besides those mentioned in the article, that are packaged in composites? If so, what are they?

_____

_____

4. What do you think should be done to encourage manufacturers to eliminate unnecessary and wasteful packaging?

_____

_____

RELATED READING: HOW GREEN ARE YOU?

Fill out the questionnaire below to find out how environmentally aware you are.

How Green Are You?

How often do you . . .	Always	Sometimes	Never
1. buy eggs and milk in cardboard cartons instead of plastic?			
2. reuse plastic and glass containers as refrigerator dishes for left-overs?			
3. take your own shopping bags to the store?			
4. avoid using a bag if you are buying only one item?			
5. buy rechargeable batteries and recharge them when needed?			
6. avoid buying "disposable" products such as razors, lighters, etc.?			
7. share your magazine subscriptions with another person?			
8. use old letters and envelopes as scrap paper?			
9. use old grocery bags for garbage bags?			
10. buy in large quantities and transfer what you buy to smaller, reusable containers?			
11. avoid buying or using styrofoam?			
12. use cloth towels and napkins instead of paper ones?			
13. buy loose fruits and vegetables instead of pre-packaged ones and avoid putting them in plastic bags before check-out?			
14. use only the exact amount of wrapping (wax paper, foil, plastic wrap) you need?			
15. write to manufacturers and complain about unnecessary or wasteful packaging?			

Scoring:
Always   = 2 points
Sometimes = 1 points
Never   = 0 points

Your Score:
25–30 Congratulations, you're already green!
15–24 Very good. You're moving in the right direction.
 5–14 You need to become more environmentally aware.
 0–4   You **really** need to increase your awareness.

SPECIAL RESEARCH ASSIGNMENT

Visit a local grocery store or supermarket and write the answers to the questions below. Then compare and discuss your findings in small groups. Report your group's conclusions to the class.

1. Name three products packaged in:

cardboard: _____   _____   _____

foil: _____   _____   _____

glass: _____   _____   _____

plastic: _____   _____   _____

polystyrene: _____   _____   _____

2. What kinds of products are NOT packaged?

_____

_____

3. Name four fruits or vegetables that come fresh, canned, and frozen
   (ex.: fresh peas, canned peas, and frozen peas):

_____   _____   _____   _____

4. Do any fresh fruits and vegetables come already wrapped in something?
   Which ones?

_____

_____

5. Name four products that are labeled "recyclable":

_____   _____   _____   _____

6. What kinds of products come in aerosol cans?

_____

_____

7. What kind of bags does the store you visited use, paper or plastic?

_____

8. Do any customers bring their own bags to the store? _____

FINAL TASK: CONDUCT A SURVEY

1. Work in groups and write a questionnaire. Make up five yes/no questions to find out people's opinions about green consumerism. Your group will interview a cross-section of people. Decide when and where you will conduct the survey, how many people you will question, who they will be, etc. When you take the survey, count the yes and no responses. Take notes on the interesting comments that people make. The following grid can be used to write your questions, count responses, and record comments.

Questions	Yes	No	Comments
Example: Are you concerned about the environmental effects of the products you buy?	⫫⫽	/	I consider myself to be very "green."
1.			
2.			
3.			
4.			
5.			

2. When your group meets again, summarize the information you have collected and prepare an oral report to present to the class. Be sure to include an introduction to your survey, a summary of the results, and a conclusion. The conclusion should include your group's interpretation of the information collected.
3. When you present your oral reports to the class, follow this procedure:
    a. One student introduces the group and gives an introduction to the survey conducted by the group.
    b. The next few students present one or two of the questions, statistics on yes and no responses, and some interesting comments made by the people who were interviewed.
    c. The last student concludes the presentation by summarizing and interpreting the information, and perhaps reacting to the results. For example, "It surprised us to learn that most people . . ."